BIPOLAR MAN

Religion, Miracles, and Disaster

ATIF YOUSAF

AuthorHouse™ UK
1663 Liberty Drive
Bloomington, IN 47403 USA
www.authorhouse.co.uk
UK TFN: 0800 0148641 (Toll Free inside the UK)
UK Local: 02036 956322 (+44 20 3695 6322 from outside the UK)

Because of the dynamic nature of the Internet, any web addresses or links contained in this book may have changed
since publication and may no longer be valid. The views expressed in this work are solely those of the author and do not
necessarily reflect the views of the publisher, and the publisher hereby disclaims any responsibility for them.

Any people depicted in stock imagery provided by Getty Images are models,
and such images are being used for illustrative purposes only.
Certain stock imagery © Getty Images.

This book is printed on acid-free paper.

ISBN: 979-8-8230-8216-7 (sc)
ISBN: 979-8-8230-8215-0 (e)

Print information available on the last page.

Published by AuthorHouse 04/13/2023

authorHOUSE®

CONTENTS

INTRODUCTION

As my title suggests, I am a sufferer of a now commonly known disease called bipolar disorder. I have been suffering from this condition since 2003. The main symptoms of bipolar are patients go through are cycles of high and low moods. The low moods may cause severe depression, which may lead to suicide. The high periods vary from hypomania, an elevated mood leading to impulsive and excessive behaviour, to psychosis, which is more severe, causing the patient to lose touch with reality.

CHAPTER 1

EARLY LIFE

I was born as the second child to parents who had emigrated from Pakistan to the United Kingdom. We lived in a suburb of Greater Manchester called Stockport; our exact location was in the Heaton Mersey Valley. My recollection of early life between the ages of four to eleven years old is that I was very happy. My father was an accountant, my mother a housewife, and they gave us a comfortable and secure household environment.

As far as I can remember, I spent much of my childhood enjoying myself playing sports. I did not attend formal clubs, but in those days, the local school allowed children to use their grounds to play football and cricket. We used to play until the sun went down. When we were between the ages of eight to ten, we would ride our bikes all over the neighbourhood and around the local area without any hesitation.

During my early teenage years, I attended Stockport School, the local comprehensive school. Here the emphasis was never on studying but more on passing the time while enjoying yourself. Out of one hundred and eighty students in the year, and only four of us were Asian, and all four Muslim. Each morning, we had assembly, and as was usual in any secondary school in that day, Christian hymns were sung. I remember attending these. Then, one day, two of the other Muslims in the year complained to me that we should not be participating in Christian worship. I continued to attend as usual; however, there were occasions when they collared me and stopped me from going in. This was the first instance I saw myself as different from other children in Stockport. The only other time was when my friend would chase me with a white paintbrush during art at primary school. This was because everybody in the school was white, and I was one of only a couple of Asian children. So, my friend used to find it funny to chase me around with a white paintbrush. It was all in fun.

When I started college, I was still aware I was Muslim. And this created restrictions for my lifestyle. While my friends were going out, getting drunk, and hanging out with girls, I played football, hockey, cricket, and squash. One time, when I ventured out with my English friends, I became aware of two distinct categories—white and brown. We went to a local ice-skating rink in Altrincham. It was notorious for being a hangout for teenagers in south Manchester. I kissed a girl, but not before head-butting her while going in for the kill. I was a laughingstock for a little while. Little did I know this would be the start of an avalanche of disastrous relationships (although that might be a slight exaggeration).

In school, my work ethic was poor. I scraped through my General Certificate of Secondary Education exams, which granted me access to A levels in maths, physics, and chemistry. I had an excellent grasp of theories when it came to chemistry and physics, but I had very little time to commit any of the information to memory, which meant my exam results were appalling. On the other hand, my mathematics was good, but I found it difficult to memorize long equations. At the same time, I was studying for my A levels, I was also resitting my GCSE in English. Two years went by. I managed to fail the English exam twice as well as all three A levels.

At this point, I didn't know which way to take my life. I knew I had to resit my A levels, but the problem was deep down within me. I knew the state education system was not the place for a student with a work ethic like mine. Basically, I was up Shit's Creek without a paddle. Now I had the tremendous task of asking my parents to fund my extra year taking A levels because of my stupidity. As previously noted, my father was an accountant who worked for his brother's firm, and my mother was a housewife, so finding an extra ten thousand pounds would be a real squeeze. However, in short, my folks agreed private education might be more suitable for my personality.

So I got in touch with Abbey Tutorial College in Manchester. I remember being interviewed by the vice principal, who conducted a little test of my knowledge about the three A levels I wished to undertake at Abbey. Dominic, the vice principal at the time, seemed encouraged by my knowledge and interview and offered me a place at Abbey. When I started Abbey, I was surprised by how focused the students were at obtaining their academic goals. Most students aimed to go into medicine or another related field, which meant achieving the highest grades.

Abbey Tutorial in those days was situated in Manchester City Centre, around the corner from Market Street and above a Pizza Hut on Fountain Street. I met some lovely people here; it was nice to be surrounded by middle-class people who had to get an education to get on in life. Everybody's parents were from a professional or business background, which is why we all probably ended up at Abbey. Life had been easy for us all, and we were having a good time, but unfortunately, we had not attained sufficient grades to keep that lifestyle going. However, we all buckled up our ideas, and most of us managed to get into our preferred university courses.

Again, though, I was one of the unlucky ones who just missed out on my preferred course. I was hoping to study dentistry at Liverpool University, for which I had an offer of two B's and a C, but I managed to get only a B and two C's. At the time, I had a backup offer from Sunderland to study pharmacy. I was reluctant to take this up, as I had set my heart upon becoming a dentist. I tried to get in through clearing to all the dental schools in the UK, but unfortunately to no avail, so I started ringing around different universities for other courses. I remember attending Manchester Metropolitan University for an interview for law with my friend Faisal. I explained to the lady interviewing me that I already had an offer to study pharmacy. She told me that was a better career for me to follow, as law was still an old boys' network. In the end, I accepted an offer from Liverpool John Moores University for pharmacy.

After getting through the clearing, I turned up to Liverpool to find accommodation. All the students were directed to a specific agent. When I got there, I met a lad called Mark, from Nottingham, who was also looking for somewhere to stay. We chatted and decided it would be a good idea to look for a place together. Then there was another lad there, Adam, from Surrey, who was also looking for accommodation. We all agreed to take a flat on the ground floor of a terrace house on Moscow Drive in the West Derby area of Liverpool. In September, I turned up to Liverpool and settled into Moscow Drive. There were four of living in the ground-floor flat—me, Mark, Adam, and another Adam from Burnley.

Above our rooms was a flat of eight students who also went to Liverpool John Moores. We often used to do things as a whole house. One night, we decided to go out to students' union, and I copped off with a girl from the pharmacy programme. We went back to her student accommodation, and I got as far as her breasts. The next day, I ended up back at my flat, and Mark asked how far I had gotten. I proceeded to tell him. He said, "What did you do that for?"

I replied, "For a pint and a half of milk!"

Then there was the pharmacy crew. As I went in for the first lecture, I was drawn to this Indian lad, Jaz. I sat next to him, and he became one of my best friends while at university. Then there was another lad, Nik, from Birmingham, who was also Indian. It was weird how the class was split. At the back was the Irish contingent. Then, just further on, were the Indians and English (plus me). Then to the right of us was a mixture of English girls and religious Pakistani girls. At the front, it was a mixture of Arabs and Chinese foreign students. It's funny, but people seemed to be just as segregated in university as they were in the real world.

I cannot remember much about studying in the first year of pharmacy. The emphasis for young undergraduates was to get drunk. We all used to go out two to three times per week. The year went by, and I got my results for the exams. As expected, I had excelled in failure. I had managed to fail seven out of eight exams for the year. Before one exam, Mark and I went to the off licence, and I had a bottle of Johnny Walker Black Label while he got his dark rum and black. We proceeded to get way past halfway through the bottles. On one occasion, we had a similar session. When I proceeded to get back from university, Mark asked me to follow him to the bathroom. He had managed to squeeze out a purple turd with all the rum and black he had drunk.

This theme continued the entire year. I was going out with pharmacy undergraduates more as we spent most of the day together between 9 a.m. and 5 p.m. The first year was full of fun, playing football and barely studying outside school hours, much to my detriment. The year had passed, but I hadn't (my exams, that is). This led me to the momentous task of resitting eight out of nine exams for the year in the summer. I remember working for Boots in the summer—my first paid-employment gig. Then I went to work for the local private hospital in Cheadle. My wages were meant to be £50 per week; however, by the end of the week, they had been doubled to £100, as my boss said she had been impressed. I do not remember being overly enthusiastic about pharmacy; however, it was growing on me. After I finished working at the private hospital, I got a job with the pharmacy department of Stepping Hill Hospital in Stockport. They were paying me, so they expected me to work; however, I was a pharmacy student, so I expected to get some clinical training while I was there. They were reluctant to do this for me, so instead of dispensing, I decided to go into stores and just chuck boxes around and have a laugh with the old men who worked there.

I passed all the resits in the summer and began my second year of pharmacy. My second year of university did not get off to a good start as I did not know whether I would return if I did not secure accommodation over the summer. Therefore, I ended up moving in with some Indian lads, one from pharmacy and the others from IT courses. Our house was an absolute shambles. I did not sign a contract before moving in, and before long, we all got fed up with the house and decided to leave without paying the rent we owed. Then, during a lecture, there was an announcement for Nik and me to see the principal of the college. I had an inkling as to the reason.

Professor Rubenstein sat us down in his office and explained it was not right what we had done. At this point, Nik became nervous and started apologizing. The professor continued, explaining it was like going for a meal and not paying, to which I responded, no, it was not; in fact, it was like tasting the starter and deciding to leave because it was not up to a good standard. The professor summarily asked us to leave his office.

I moved into a flat with a Pakistani lad, Waseem. The flat had two large double bedrooms and a nice large lounge with a built-in kitchen. However, I found living with Asians to be uncomfortable, as they took liberties and did not respect boundaries. At the same time, it was a lot of fun living with Waseem. We would go out around three times each week. Thus, another year passed. I managed to pass most of my exams and had only two resits in the summer.

CHAPTER 2

LIZ

My third year at university began, and this year, I moved back in with Mark, Lorna, and a few others from year one. This was the year I met Liz Fellows. We met on a Wednesday evening at Friday's nightclub, underneath the Adelphi Hotel. I ended the night taking her number, and we started dating. Liz was an English and music student at Liverpool Hope University. She was a typically fit bird, pleasing to the eye, with a great body. It turned out Liz was Catholic, which was good, as at that time, being Muslim, I believed in God, but it was good that we had this commonality. The year went by quickly, and I graduated with a third, which was about right for the effort I had put into my studies. However, I was not that bothered, as I had a job lined up with Lloyds pharmacy regardless of what grade I achieved in my degree. I had been given my preregistration job at Hull, but as I was now dating Liz, who was in Liverpool for another year, I wanted to be closer to her. So, after some negotiation with Lloyds, they switched my pharmacy training to Widnes.

Getting used to working life after studying was difficult, and on the weekends, the partying would continue. One night, I was staying over at the house of a preregistration tutor, Sue. We had arranged a night out to Liverpool. Liz met up with us, and we had a good night. Then we went back to Sue's house in Warrington. Shortly afterwards, Sue left the Lloyds, and I would be transferred to the Wirral. My tutor was a gentleman, Paul, who eventually left to work in Australia. This led me to my third preregistration placement, with Mr Wilson. Liz and I were getting on well until one night, when he and I were out with my brother, Zak, and cousin, Hamad, in Liverpool. We had gone to the Blue Angel nightclub; a flatmate of mine was there, and I ended up snogging her. Also in the club were a couple of Liz's friends, which meant I had been caught out.

On Monday, I got a telephone call from Liz simply asking me to pick up my belongings from her house. My initial reaction was to ask Mr Wilson for a few hours off so I could sort out this horrific mess. I proceeded to Liz's house, where she was in a rage, having torn up pictures of us together. My initial feeling was, *How can this be the end of us?* But it was for now. I returned to the pharmacy and completed my shift.

After a lot of grovelling, Liz and I started to spend more time together, and after a couple of months, we were back together. However, something had changed, and I was suddenly on the back foot. She had the upper hand, which meant we tended to do things she wanted.

Liz wanted to do a publishing course in Leeds, so after my preregistration was complete, we moved into a flat together in Horsforth. I kept working for Lloyds but on a permanent locum basis. The money was good for that time, and Liz and I decided to get married. Looking back on the situation, my parents made quite the exception allowing us to get married, as we were living in sin. At the time, they were not in favour of the marriage—to the point where they discouraged others from attending the wedding. The more people were averse to our wedding, the more difficult it became, and at one point, we both probably wondered whether we were doing the right thing. My parents were not the only ones with reservations; Liz's mother (Julia) and their priest also objected. Perhaps our marriage was doomed from the off, but at that age, you do not listen to others, so we went ahead with our wedding.

In the end, the wedding was attended by both of our families, and we had a great time. The first day was the registration at the Bridlington registry office, followed that same day by the Muslim ceremony at Bridlington Links Golf Club. After this, we had the morning breakfast and an evening do. The following day, as we could not invite all our friends to the Friday main event, we had another function at Leeds, where we were living at the time. This was a formal event but much more relaxed, without any formal religious proceedings. The following day, my parents held a function for all their family who could not attend the other two functions. All in all, we had three days of ceremonies and celebrations. At the time, I was working for Lloyds as a locum and could only afford to take a week off, which we spent in Paris. To be honest, we could have done with a week on the beach, as we came back exhausted from sightseeing.

After returning from our honeymoon, we moved into a brand-new flat in Rodley on the bank of the Leeds and Liverpool Canal. After about six months working in graphic design (producing business cards), Liz realized she had to pursue another career. So, after formally declaring she would never go into teaching, she enrolled in the PGCE course. So, as Liz was going back, I decided to enrol into an MSc course in Prescribing Sciences at Robert Gordon University Aberdeen. The course in Aberdeen was mainly distance learning, with a week in residence each year for the two years. During one of the residential weeks, we had to look into drug-adverse reactions, and I remember getting enthusiastic about mine. The long shot of it was I got to the bottom of the pharmacokinetics of adverse reactions with the help of a few lecturers. However, this enthusiasm in pharmacology got me thinking about going back to university to do an MPhil. Two things deterred me from taking up the offer at Robert Gordon's University. First, the pharmaceutical chemist who had helped me solve the drug-adverse reaction problem enlightened me that after the age of thirty, it is difficult to work in the area of drug design and formulation. Second, Liz explained that I did not like studying and would be wasting my time. In hindsight, she probably did not want to relocate to Scotland.

Liz completed her PGCE and got a job in south Leeds, and I had come to the end of my diploma. I had been developed into a clinical pharmacist, and now, I needed to find a job to reflect my newly acquired knowledge and skills. So, I applied for a post as a clinical-practice pharmacist at Sheffield South East PCT. I managed to get the application form in just in time and was offered an interview. The interview consisted of three parts: patient consultation, presentation, and interview. I performed very well at the patient consultation and interview, but my presentation skills needed improvement. The boss, Steve, was sufficiently impressed and called me the next day to offer me the job. I was over the moon, as this was the perfect opportunity to be paid to use my clinical skills and intellect rather than have my performance based on the number of prescriptions I dispensed.

So, after arriving in the lovely city of Leeds in 1998, in the summer of 2002, we were on the move again, to South Yorkshire. The housing market was booming, and the in thing to do was to remortgage one property and buy another with the equity that had been released. As anyone will know, moving to a new house is a stressful time, and until you get the keys, you fear that something will go wrong. For me, the fear was remortgaging the flat in Rodley so we afford to buy a lovely three-bed cottage in Aston, Sheffield. For the first couple of months, while working in Sheffield, both Liz and I were commuted from Leeds. Finally, we got the keys to our lovely cottage on the outskirts of Sheffield. It took a little time to adjust to the new house. It had thick stone walls, which kept it cool in the summer, but in the winter, it was very difficult to heat. In the autumn, when we moved in—I don't know whether it was the stress of moving to a new house and starting a new job or the small windows—but I felt tired all the time and regularly fell asleep about nine o'clock in the evenings.

Everything seemed to be going well with life—I was happily married and had a good job. Then came the first sign that I was not invincible. It was 24 December, and I was in Manchester for Christmas Eve. I had gone out with my dad for a couple of pints, after which I was supposed to play five-a-side football with my younger brother, Wasif, and his friends. So, we went to play football, and I ended up going for a ball when two opposition players tackled me at the same time. The outcome was a fractured fibula in two places and a dislocated foot (sitting at a right angle to where it should have been). While my brother, a fourth-year medic, sussed out the situation, I had a look and shouted, "Get an ambulance!"

The ambulance crew came after about ten minutes and discovered I did not have a pulse in my foot; therefore, with only gas and air, they had to pull and twist the foot back into place. It was the most painful experience of my life.

To add insult to injury, I had to Christmas morning make my way to the in-laws in Bridlington. I would have preferred to stay in Manchester; however, as my wife was a devout Christian, I would really be in the doghouse had I not agreed to make the trip. So, my brother took me halfway on Christmas morning, and Liz came and picked me up from Goole in Yorkshire. We made it back to Bridlington and had Christmas dinner with family in a pub. After enduring the festivities, all I wanted to do was put my feet up, but as usual, Liz had other plans— going round all the shops in Bridlington. The sensible thing would have been to stay home and nurse the ankle, but no—I had to endure being pushed round Bridlington town centre in a wheelchair. For some of the time, they left me out in the cold, and as a result, I ended up getting cellulitis in the broken leg.

The pain was immense, and each time I moved my leg, I felt liquid move through my leg, causing pain. I went to see Dr Wynn at Heaton Mersey Medical Practice, who gave me strong pain killers and antibiotics. Then, after the Christmas period, I went back to Sheffield. I was waiting for my parents to visit me one day. When they arrived, I was upstairs, and in a hurry to get down the stairs, I fell. The next day, I had another X-ray of the leg and was informed that the fracture was out of position—and there was also a fracture further up, which had not been diagnosed. This meant the orthopaedic surgeon was eager for me to get it operated on and have a screw put in to keep the ankle joint in place to prevent arthritis in later life. He also explained this would mean I could play football again. I was reluctant to have the operation because it would mean at least another eight weeks in plaster, which would add up to twelve in total. I was also wary, as I had started a new job only a few months before and did not want to take prolonged time off. In the end, I had the operation and was back at work within two weeks. The plaster was still on, and my place of work arranged for taxis to ferry me around, along with friends from work helping out where they could. I remember sitting in a different doctor's surgery office and seeing patients with a broken leg. The first patient would let in the next one.

CHAPTER 3

TURKEY

Apart from the broken leg and a few failed exams along the way, my life had been plain sailing. We had a comfortable lifestyle, usually with two holidays abroad each year. I had always been a thinker in my own time, wondering what makes the world go round. As a younger man, I always concluded it was money. I was pretty happy as a twenty-seven-year-old, at which time, I was still a Muslim. So, as we were looking for holiday destinations, I suggested to Liz that we try Turkey. She was not too keen on the idea, but she agreed, so we ended up getting a last-minute holiday to Icmeler, a resort on the Mediterranean Coast of Turkey. As Liz worked as a primary school teacher, we could take our holiday only during the hottest season. The temperature was around 35 degrees Celsius in the shade. The transfer from the airport to the holiday resort of Icmeler was about two hours. In the heat, the journey seemed to last for hours. We finally got to the hotel and unpacked quickly, then headed down to the pool for a lazy day. On the first night, we went out for dinner, then came back to the hotel to have a few drinks by the poolside bar. Liz decided to go to bed, and then I started to talk to people at the bar.

I got to taking to two beautiful girls who must have been in their early twenties. We got on the subject of faith, and they both told me they were atheists. In my slightly drunken state, I thought I would try to rectify this situation. So, while talking to these lovely girls from Holland, I asked them if they could close their eyes. Then, one by one, I put the palm of my hand about one centimetre away from their face without touching them. After I had done this to each one, I asked whether they could feel anything with their eyes shut. They both told me they could feel something, but it was not me touching their faces. They felt a presence, however, and could tell there was something very close to them.

"If I was not I touching you," I said, "and you had your eyes closed, how do you explain what you felt when I put my hand up towards you?"

They were stumped and had no answer to give me. We got talking about God. I don't remember the exact conversation went, but there was a consensus that none of us could explain what had happened; it was phenomenon inexplicable by the usual laws of science. All in all, I do not believe I converted anyone to my faith, but at least now they were thinking about the phenomenon of God.

Unfortunately, the next day, there was a young boy at pool who had been up the night before, and he accused me of chatting up the two girls. This caused negativity between the two girls and Liz, which was a shame, because they were too of only a few in our age bracket. We did, however, get talking to another couple our age and spent time with them going out for meals and having drinks by the poolside.

I remember talking to the people behind the bar, who were watching people all day, and on a number of occasions, they must have heard me preaching, not exactly ramming any religion down anyone's throat but just leisurely talking—not about my faith, which was Islam at the time, just talking about God in general. The people behind the bar were Muslims and said I had a good way of talking to people and people tended to listen to me. I found this reassuring, and at the same time, a sense of euphoria hit me. Maybe it was God's calling for me to speak about him.

Also staying at the hotel was a family—a husband and wife in their mid-forties who had brought their fourteen-year-old daughter. The daughter was accompanied by her boyfriend. When I heard this young couple was sharing a room, I was quite taken aback. I had had quite a conservative upbringing, and back at home, the age of consent was sixteen. This situation stood quite uncomfortably with me, and I made this known to the parents of the young girl. In hindsight, it was none of my business, but we are all prone to revealing our feelings at times.

Obviously, this girl took a disliking to me, and she kept her distance. Then one day, while I was on the aftershocks, I decided it would be fair to buy this young lady a few drinks for judging her. She happily accepted the drinks but still kept her distance. The time had come for the two Dutch girls to go home, so as they were leaving, I went over and apologized to them for refusing to talk to them after that night. They asked why Liz had taken it so badly and what that stupid boy had said. They asked whether I had betrayed her before, and I had to confess that when I was at university, I had kissed another girl, so she might have a few trust issues. They said it was a shame because they had enjoyed my company that evening.

It had been a great holiday so far, but what happened next would change my entire life. While I was playing on the water slide, I had a high-speed clash of heads with another man. Despite the likely concussion that resulted, what followed was bizarre. I had bought a couple bottles of Aftershock and put them behind the bar. I was offering everybody drinks, not feeling quite right. Then the fourteen-year-old girl who I had fallen out with came over to me and asked me, "Can you still call yourself a Muslim what after what they did on 9/11 in New York?"

I immediately answered with a resounding, "No!"

"Well, then, you're just a really good man then!" she replied.

This was a massive turning point in my life. I was no longer a Muslim. My whole identity had been changed. I still believed in God, but what now?

I remember then going to dinner with my wife at the restaurant on the hotel grounds. For argument's sake, I counted my money before the meal and had about 200 lire, which would have been sufficient to pay the bill. However, when the bill came and I came to pay for the food, the total was 180 lire, and I was only had 150. I counted the money two or three times, and I came up short each time.

One of the waiters asked me "What do you want?"

I stood up and said, "I want everyone to be equal!"

A million thoughts were going through my mind. I knew there was something wrong but could not identify what it was. At first, I thought my drink had been spiked.

I got up from the table and threw my wallet with all its contents into the pool. As I made my way to the hotel room, I shouted, "You should all be Muslim!" I was still clearly confused about my own faith and clinging on to Islam as I had been practising this religion for twenty-eight years. When you have deep faith in God and have been brought up as a Muslim, it is complicated to part with such beliefs.

Back in our room, I went into a state of panic, thinking I was a special sort of person who had a close link with God. As I lay there, I thought I was going to die. Lying next to my wife, I confessed my sins to her as I thought I was going to die and wanted to leave a clean slate and be forgiven for them before the end.

Liz was trying to calm me down and get me to go to sleep. I was clearly agitated, and Liz, frightened, performed a gesture over my head, what seemed like the sign of the cross, thus baptizing me.

The next morning, I got up, and my wallet had been retrieved from the pool with all its contents. When I counted the money, there were 200 lire. This baffled me, and I thought someone had spiked my drink. I was furious and confused. I just wanted to get out of there and told Liz to help me pack our bags so we could get to the airport. I remember saying to her, "How would you like it if you had been drugged? Would you want to stay here? Anything could have happened to you."

She got upset and agreed to pack our bags and leave for the airport.

Before going to the airport, we got some money out on the credit card and bought a rug, which we had previously decided to do. We purchased some bottles of Coke for the journey, which were in glass bottles. After this, we returned to the hotel to pick up our bags. On the way out, we said goodbye to various people who did not understand why we were leaving early. In the taxi on the way to the airport, I remember thinking about the events of the previous couple of weeks. I remember feeling very confused. Thoughts were running through my mind. At one point, I thought I was Jesus, who come had returned. My thoughts were all linked to the ideation of making the world a better place—fair for all who lived on the earth.

I could not figure out if I was Jesus or some other prophet, but I had the sense I was really close to God and on earth was the closest person, and God wanted to use me for his mission to make the world a better place. My first thought was that I had been sent to help those who live in Africa, as growing up, we were told they were the most underprivileged people on earth and had witnessed the devastating famines in Ethiopia. I had a sense of euphoria and thought the taxi driver also knew who I was, a prophet related to Jesus or Jesus himself. Tears streamed down my cheeks, as it was emotionally confusing, particularly the thought of having my drink spiked, which, in turn, could have caused me to be confused.

When we got to the airport, I was still thinking I was a prophet. Knowing that the driver knew this as well, I was under the impression he would not want to charge us for the ride, so I just got out of the car and with the glass bottles of Coke we had bought earlier. After leaving the car, I started to smash the bottles on the pavement. In my head, I believed I needed to do this so people could follow in my footsteps and replicate this as an act of worship—some sort of ritual. This freaked out the driver of the vehicle, not to mention my wife. Eventually, I handed the money over to the taxi driver, and we proceeded to the airport.

Once we got inside the airport, there was no ticket office open or opportunity to get a flight back to England. I became furious at this and, without thinking of the consequences, picked up a bollard used as a dividing line and threw it about fifteen feet up into the air, where it smashed the glass wall of the airport. I was arrested and taken to a police officer's office. They tried to question me, but I was not saying much, and I was clearly ill. Liz was trying to tell them that this was totally out of character and confirmed that I was indeed ill. I recall hearing voices. The airport did not seem busy, but I could hear flights coming in. Bizarrely, I thought I could hear one of my cousins, Sofia.

At this point, I thought everyone should know I was a prophet and acknowledge this. Thoughts were racing through my mind; I remember flicking a pen lid high into the air and hitting a window high up. The police officer questioned how I had managed to flick the lid so high and so far, but I kept quiet. Eventually, Liz convinced them of my illness. They said I needed to pay for the broken window and arranged for an ambulance to take me to a hospital. I got in the ambulance, and they put me on a drip. I knew this would contain medication to calm me down, so I looked, and sure enough, the drip contained some sort of benzodiazepine, a sedative.

Knowing that the drip would slow down my racing thoughts which were getting away from me, I reached out and pinched the line to slow down the delivery of the drug into my vein. Liz did not know how to cope on her own and called my dad back in England. She needed help with me and asked my dad to come out and help get me home. Realizing what had happened, I calmed down, wanting only to get out of the hospital. They made me stay one night in hospital, and Liz stayed with me in the room. All the time in hospital, I could not understand why. I realized something was wrong, but I could not get these racing thoughts from outside my head. At the same time, everything seemed so real— as if I had been put on earth to lead people, to bring all humanity to a state of equality with each other.

I suppose I was suffering from delusions of grandeur, symptoms that commonly manifest in patients who suffer from bipolar disorder. Liz, struggling to cope with what was happening, contacted my father. So, my father and Uncle Anwar flew out to Marmaris, where I had been taken into hospital. They arrived on the day I was due to be released. It was nice for both of us to have support from others in a foreign country. Upon his arrival, my father also seemed a little shaken up, perhaps because he had suffered through a similar experience when he was younger. In fact, I discovered, he did himself take medication for schizophrenia.

After I was discharged from hospital, we had to find a hotel for us all. We managed to find one close to the centre of Marmaris. Sitting in the lounge of the room we had hired out, I drank a bottle of water. On the back of the bottle was a symbol of a building with five pillars, one of which was broken. This was a sign I was at the end of my Muslim faith. I was also convinced people could hear my thoughts and that I could communicate to them by thinking and they would respond using facial expressions. You could say I was experiencing signs and symptoms of schizophrenia. However, already knowing this disease was in my family, I remained quiet about the thoughts racing through my mind.

That night, we took a walk through the town centre and ended up going for a curry as our evening meal. Afterwards, while walking through the town, everything seemed very quiet and quaint. Then, as we were walking past a man standing next to the pavement, he asked me, "Are you making this up?" or something to that effect. Liz overheard this and asked me what he had said. I replied I had not heard him. This was just another sign that people knew I was a prophet but were not telling me. I do not know what Liz was thinking or if she had noticed that people were acting peculiarly towards us.

CHAPTER 4

BI-POLAR - MANIA

The next day, we were to travel back to Manchester. We were unable to get the same flight, so Liz and I took our scheduled flight back, and my father and uncle caught a later flight, which would take them to Glasgow. They would then have to hire a car to drive back to Manchester. We boarded our plane, and on our way back, we sat behind a lady with a four-year-old girl. The girl was quite playful, and at first, the flight seemed to go by quickly. Then, about two and a half hours in, I began to panic. I thought our flight had been diverted to another place and that we should have been home by now. I did not realize the return flight would be four and a half hours, and paranoia was kicking in again. I just could not understand what was going on; either my mind was playing games after my drink was spiked, or it was the bang on the head, or people were lying to me and refusing to acknowledge I was earth's latest prophet. I had no idea what this meant for me or anyone else on earth, so, without any concrete evidence that I was, in fact, a prophet, I said nothing.

I was confused and annoyed. Either my thoughts were very deluded—in which case, I had gone nuts—or God had some greater plan for me.

We soon landed in Manchester. As soon as we got into the airport, I think Liz felt a little bit more at home, and she expressed annoyance with me. On home soil, she became a bit bossy, which was probably justified considering the stress she had endured over the previous few days. We got back to my parents' house in Stockport, and considering everything that had happened, I thought it better not to go straight back to work. So, I remember calling in sick that night, and I said I would be back in the following afternoon; I would spend only one day in Stockport and wait for my father and uncle to get back from Turkey, via Glasgow.

The following day, I got to work about midday. Things had seemed to settle down a little in my mind. I had not told anyone at work what had happened in Turkey. I was glad to get back to work and reality. I threw myself back into work at the deep end and had registered to do a supplementary prescribing course for pharmacists at Bradford University with one of my colleagues, who would also be attending. Shefali, was one of the senior pharmacists. During the first week back at work, I was busy going about my medication review clinics in five GP practices I worked with. For my course, Dr Anita Campbell, one of the senior partners at Richmond health centre in Sheffield, would be my clinical tutor.

Before I started my clinical training with Anita, Shefali and I had to attend a week's course in Bradford. I decided that rather than commute, I would stay in university accommodation. The week seemed to go by fine, with no major hiccups. Around this time, the Black Eyed Peas had released the song "Where Is the

Love?" For some reason, this song just resonated with me, and I had put it on my car on repeat. Then, at the weekend, Liz and I headed to Manchester for the weekend. Something happened where Liz thought she was spending too much time with my family, and she decided to spend some time with her father, who also lived in Manchester and not too far from my parents.

Our family was gathering at one of my aunties' houses, around the corner from my parents' house. While there, we all sat around, and I had the feeling again that I could communicate to people in my family without speaking. Then I recall we were seated, and one of my female cousins' knees touched mine. I felt my personal space was invaded, so I got up and went home, where my dad was sitting in the front room. For some reason, I remember calling my younger brother, Wasif, who was at university, summoning him home for some unknown reason. However, he called my father back, and my dad responded, "It's OK. You don't need to come. I've not asked you to. For some reason, the paranoia was getting worse. I thought everyone knew I was a prophet but concealing this from me.

Liz had gone home from her dad's house, and my eldest brother, Saqib, gave me a lift back to Sheffield. When we arrived in Sheffield, I opened the door and went upstairs. Liz was dying her hair. For some reason, I asked her not to dye her hair, as I saw this as an act of changing her physical appearance, which, for me run counter to my faith, like getting a tattoo. My brother went home that night, and the next day, I would be starting my clinical training with Dr Anita Campbell at Richmond Medical Centre.

For some reason, I could not get to sleep that night. Part of me was excited about starting this new course, and the biggest part of the problem was that I was suffering from a mental-health problem. The night seemed to last forever and did not get a wink of sleep. Even Liz had a poor night's sleep, as she would wake up occasionally and ask me why I was not sleeping. Eventually, our alarm went off, and we both got ready for work. For some reason that day, I felt the need to make Liz's sandwich—probably because we had been away all weekend, there were only fish sticks in the fridge, so I made what must have been the worst sandwich ever. Liz, seeing there must be something wrong but needing to go to work, left the house, as I did, each of us going in our own direction. I had a little MR2 Toyota sports car, and I drove erratically to work. When I came to the health centre at Richmond, I swung my car round and crashed into the gates. I abandoned my car at the gates and proceeded to walk into the surgery.

As I entered the surgery, I asked where Dr Campbell was and proceeded into her consultation room. I do not know whether Anita could tell something was wrong, but looking back at the situation, I was not well. She started examining a patient, and it seemed she was asking me where I thought this gentleman's problem was. The gentleman was obese, and she seemed to be asking me whether his problem was mental. Regarding his obese stature, I said, "This where his medical problems lie." I just walked out of the surgery, got into my car, and started driving toward my house.

My thoughts were running wild, and I was driving my sports car on the roads as if I were on a racetrack. Suddenly, I got the urge to go back to Manchester, so I proceeded towards the motorway. When I joined the motorway, I got into the third lane and then, for some reason, I changed to the second and started swaying in the middle lane. Then I stopped my car in the middle of the motorway, and all the traffic stopped behind me, and the motorway came to a standstill. Suddenly, a policeman came to the side of my car and instructed me to pull over onto the hard shoulder. All the while, I was playing the Black Eyed Peas single "Where Is the Love?"

I got into the back of the police car, and the police were asking me questions, but for some reason, I was not answering the two officers in the car. When we got to the police station, I was put into a cell at what must have been 10 a.m. My time in the cell is a bit of a blur now, but I remember I was still having racing thoughts through my mind. For some reason, I was not afraid of what was happening. I just felt so close to God. It took them the best part of the day to interview me. However, in the end, they had me seen by an on-call psychiatrist. After a short time, I was taken out of my cell, then transferred to the psychiatric unit at Rotherham General Hospital.

CHAPTER 5

FIRST HOSPITAL ADMISSION

To be honest, this hospital stay was so long ago it is a bit of a blur, but I remember entering the ward. At the time, I was still quite ill., I accepted treatment, which was in the form of a drug called olanzapine. The dose I was given was 20 mg. At this time, Dr Abed the consultant psychiatrist, diagnosed my condition as bipolar disorder. I did not know much about the condition. While in hospital, I spent a lot of time talking to the staff. Engagement with patients was low. I would stay up late, and my sleep patterns were all over the place; I needed only a few hours of sleep each night.

I remember at one point being interviewed by Dr Abed and his assistant. They were interviewing me and asking questions like, "If you are a prophet, are you going to start a new religion?" I remember answering there was no need for a new religion, as Jesus was Jewish and we should all follow in his footsteps and guidance. They came back at me another time with a statement. Dr Abed said he and his assistants were Catholics, so why didn't I change my religion to theirs? My reaction to them was, "No. Jesus said, 'Do as the Jews say, not do.'" For me at that time, the one true religion was Judaism, which I knew Jesus followed.

To be honest, I did not know much about Catholicism or Christianity. I knew about Jesus from primary school and from going to church with Liz, but even then, when I would go to church, I would not pay attention. I was there in body, not in mind.

On this first admission to hospital, they ran comprehensive tests—from CT scans to a lumber punch. The doctor who did the lumber punch said I was one of the easiest patients he had performed the procedure on. I had not even flinched. However, after all the tests were done, which took about two weeks, they found no physical abnormality. My initial thought while in hospital was, "Why me?" I found it difficult to come to terms with the diagnosis of bipolar disorder. At first, during the acute illness, time went by quickly as the euphoria was keeping depression at bay. I had suffered from one manic episode, which was being treated with 20 mg of olanzapine daily.

Olanzapine (originally branded Zyprexa) is an antipsychotic medication used to treat schizophrenia and bipolar disorder. It is usually classed with *atypical* (the newer generation of) antipsychotics. It appears to have slightly greater effectiveness in treating schizophrenia (especially the negative symptoms) and a lower risk of causing movement disorders than typical antipsychotics. Olanzapine, however, has a higher risk of causing metabolic side effects, like weight gain and type-2 diabetes, than typical antipsychotics.

While in hospital in hospital, I had not noticed the effects of the medication because most of the side effects occur with prolonged use. Olanzapine, as with all other antipsychotic medication, works by reducing the amount of dopamine in the brain. Dopamine is the neurotransmitter in the brain associated with heightened euphoric moods and pleasurable sensations, such as heightened sexual function. It is thought that in patients with schizophrenia and bipolar disorder, there are increased levels of dopamine, which are part of the central nervous system.

From my experience taking these drugs, the side effects are horrendous. For most patients who suffer and require treatment with these drugs, there is a massive impact on body weight, especially with olanzapine. From my experience, even at low doses, there is significant morbidity. I will talk a little later of the vast negative effects these drugs have had on my life.

While in hospital, I was very fortunate to have my wife and parents visiting regularly. Liz would visit every day after finishing work at her primary school, and my parents would visit every other day from Manchester. This was an isolated part of my life. Before now, I was used to being around other people most of the time, be they friends at university, family at home, or, in more recent times, colleagues and patients. When I was at home, I had the full attention of my wife. So, suddenly having no one to talk to was very unusual. On the ward, I was reluctant to talk to other patients. I likely had a superiority complex towards them, because during my working life, I had been used to giving patients advice about their illness. Then, suddenly, I found myself mixed in with them on a psychiatric ward. I was fully aware of where I was and knew I had to toe the line with whichever medical treatment they would issue me. Otherwise, I would hinder my own progress getting out of this wretched place.

Looking back on my stays in hospital, the majority the time, I was on a secure ward, and it felt like I had been imprisoned. However, while at Rotherham General Hospital, I spent a lot of time talking to nurses, as I still considered myself a health professional. I would be suffering from insomnia and would stay up talking to the nurses throughout the night—or at least until the early hours of the morning. However, I did not realize this was probably hindering my exit from hospital, as it was one of the symptoms of hypomania in bipolar affective disorder.

While in hospital, I found it difficult to occupy my free time; it was a very surreal and artificial set-up, without any work to do and no structure to the day. I recall my favorite way to spend the day was listening to music. My favourite song was by the band Simple Red, "Home." The chorus goes something, "Think cool, and it should be over for a long for a feeling of home. Real life depicted in song, loving memory, a place where a yearn to belong." This song resonated with my emotions, as I yearned to be home with my wife.

The hospital organized some activities, which were run by the occupational therapists, who seemed to be the nicest people on the ward one encountered. This was quite a relaxing time, and I remember in one of the art classes drawing a picture of houses, which were all the same, not too dissimilar to the house I grew up, in Heaton Mersey, Stockport. That I drew clouds with a silver lining. What was going through my mind at time was that everyone should have an equal upbringing with equal opportunities. However, I was unaware of how this would be achieved. So, for now, I drew a picture of the ideal house—a modest detached home that everybody could afford, resembling the house I grew up in. I I knew they could fill children's heart with love and laughter and leaving them not longing for anything.

Then, one day, as my parents were visiting and by my bedside a was laying there, in conscious but with a feeling of vulnerability and then suddenly. I started to hallucinate. I remember it vividly. I started seeing people's faces flicker before me, one by one, changing at a vigorous pace. There must have been a hundred faces I saw, none of which were familiar. Once this happened, I knew something supernatural was going on, and my trancelike mood continued. What happened next was frightening at the time but also exonerating, leaving me feeling spiritually cleansed.

I remember to this day, as I lay in my bed, wondering if I was having an exorcism of demons from my mind. To this day, I have never told anyone what happened, and I wonder if anyone else has had such an experience. As I lay in bed taking shallow breaths, I felt my body and mind cleansing themselves, as if demons were being cleansed from my body. As I lay there, totally unable to emerge from the trance, I started to see demons released from my body and floating from my head and chest area towards my feet, then finally disappearing. This experience did not last very long, only about five minutes. As each demon left my body, I felt a weight lifted from my soul. I know this sounds like a whole load of cod's wallop, but I assure you, this is the truth. Once the "exorcism of demons" had occurred, I was left exhausted and just lay there, unable to say anything to anyone else. I had the sense that my mother knew what was going at the time, but nobody in my family has ever talked about it, and I am positive they did not see the demons that were released from my body.

I knew before this point that God had chosen me for his work—first, the euphoria of being a prophet in Turkey, and now, this cleansing of my soul. I did not tell anybody what I was going through, as I could not prove what had happened. Even with my wife, I was unable to share this. I could hardly believe what was happening myself, let alone explain it to others. At the time, I put it down to illness and hallucinations. I could not scientifically explain what was happening to me.

I had always believed in God and wondered why I was being chosen or picked by God. Anyway, I had to send all these things to the back of my mind, as I had bills to pay and a wife to look after. This was my first time in hospital, and I had not been made aware of the implications of being on a section. Either this had not been properly explained to me, or there had been no explanation. I remember, one day, when I had been afforded some leave from the ward. I used the opportunity to buy some flowers for my wife and then proceeded to hire a taxi and make my way to the school where she was working. She was shocked to see me and knew I had left the hospital without their permission. She had to get the head teacher to take charge of her class while she drove me back to Rotherham General Hospital. Another day, after Liz had had a meeting with the treating doctors, she asked me what I wanted. And at the time, I remember answering a saxophone. For some reason, I had a genuine urge to play the saxophone. But as with many things in life, I never got a saxophone, and to this day, I cannot read music or play any musical instrument.

After about four to six weeks in hospital, I was discharged home. After my release from hospital, I thought it would be a simple procedure to go back to work and lead a normal life. All I wanted was to be back at my desk, helping patients, but here I was, stuck at home. I had to go through the rigorous procedures of occupational health at Sheffield Hallam Hospital before I could get back to work. So, in the meantime, I had all this spare time on my hands and no idea what to do. There were only so many times you could go down to the driving range, especially when a starter at golf.

Basically, I was left with a sickening void in my life and started to question, *Why me?* What had I done wrong in my life to receive this slow death sentence? The more I read about bipolar disorder, the more determined I was to stop taking the medication. I was on a very high dose of onlazapine, and this made me feel very lethargic, and I completely lost the ability to laugh. This existence was soul-destroying. I had been a busy professional, and suddenly, I had to take a back seat and just twiddle my thumbs, day in and day out. Each night, my wife would give me my medication. From early in my treatment, I had taken a dislike to the medication. It was just so debilitating. Psychiatric medication, on the whole, is very strong, with debilitating side effects. So, I was in a horrible situation, where I had been given medication to treat my illness, which made me more ill than the condition itself.

CHAPTER 6

THE VOID

My days were filled with a massive void. Liz would get up at about seven o'clock in the morning and leave the house and not return until around six in the evening. During this time, I had no desire to do anything and getting out of bed was a massive struggle. I remember that my brother Wasif had got me a PlayStation 2 with a car-racing game, but I was never one to play computer games. Even though so many seem to thrive wasting hours playing these games, I could barely play them for half an hour. And do not get me started on daytime television.

The inevitable happened. Liz could see I was not my usual self, so she had me see my psychiatrist, and immediately, I was put on antidepressants. I suppose they call it bipolar for a reason: you have amazing highs and then a very depressing low, where you have to make the best of the diabolical situation left in the aftermath of the madness. Looking back on the situation now, I was depressed, but it was my circumstances that made me feel so low. Having worked for the past few years, never being out of work, being suddenly at home without anything to do was disturbing. I was also worried I had started my prescribing course, which at the time I was thoroughly excited about as this was the first cohort of pharmacists who were going through the training.

Something inside me had changed, be it the depression of bipolar disorder alone or the amalgamating effects due to the medication. At the time, I felt sorry for myself, wallowing in regret that I had been diagnosed with bipolar disorder and was suffering from such an ailment. Weeks went by, and I had to push for my doctor to send reports back to occupational health. Once you have a diagnosis of a severe mental health disorder, there is stigma that surrounds it, whether people want to believe it or not. People's perception of you changes, whether they admit it or not. People can cope with physical illness, but with mental illness, the patient may lose touch with reality or act erratically. This sticks in people, however forgiving they may be. They will perceive you in a different light from the beginning of your illness. Part of the problem is that it is challenging for people with mental health issues to open up about what is going through their minds, which is a shame because most people with schizophrenia-type symptoms have a great story to tell. Some of the hallucinations are magnificent and seem so real until you have time to reflect and realize that the experience was your mind playing tricks on you.

The problem with being a pharmacist and having influence over people's health and access to drugs is that everybody is extra cautious. In my eyes, this amounts to disability discrimination.

Eventually, my consultant and occupational health signed off on my return to work, which was a great relief. However, back at work, it was not all smooth sailing. Before I resumed my clinical duties, I was subjected to monitoring and extra tests. Also, I was still suffering from depression and found it difficult to concentrate. My manager asked me how I had spent the day, and I replied that I had spent mostly catching up on emails. He was not too happy to hear this.

My performance at work was below par, and management got human resources involved. I remember being under extra pressure to perform, but the drugs I had been given were highly sedating, caused lethargy and sluggish thinking. As mine was a clinical role, the ability to manipulate data and think on my feet, with problem-solving ideas, was critical to my job, and I greatly struggled. Gradually, my dose of olanzapine was reduced, and I managed to wean off the antidepressants.

A breaking point came around May that year, when I visited my parents at home. My brother, Wasif was studying medicine and planned to go to Australia to catch up with some of his friends, who had gone there for their electives. We got talking, and somehow, we made a plan for my older brother, Saqib, and me to join him on his trip. For some bizarre reason, without first checking with my line manager, I decided to take four weeks off work and go down under.

Although we were going on holiday within two weeks, I needed approval from work. I had already booked my flight, which cost nearly a thousand pounds. My boss was little more than concerned by my actions. However, given the rough ride I'd had recently with my health, he decided to grant my leave due to special circumstances. This turned out to be one of the best holidays of my life. We ended up scuba diving on the barrier reef and taking a road trip from Cairns to Brisbane. We did all the usual stuff down the Gold Coast, Cairns, the Whitsunday Islands, and Frazer Island. As soon as I boarded the flight to Brisbane, I decided to stop taking my medication.

However, on holiday, I was still suffering from the side effects of the medication, including increasingly drowsiness and narcolepsy. This trip was a real boost. It got me out of the rut of being on medication and the feeling I was not stuck in a rut and hampered by my diagnosis. The highlight of my trip was scuba diving on the barrier reef. At first, we had some in-pool training for the PADI course, which was spent half the time in the pool and half the time on board a ship. However, I stumbled on the first hurdle. During the first morning, we were due to have a medical, and I filled out my paperwork honestly, which meant I declared being on olanzapine (20 mg daily) as well as fluoxetine (40 mg daily).

To my horror, I was pulled aside by the doctor and told he was unable to sign my medical fitness form as I was fluoxetine 40 mg, a high dose, which led to increased risk of seizure, which could be dangerous underwater. I was gutted. Anyhow, both Saqib and I quit the course and decided to go on a live board out to the Barrier Reef. We were on board for four days; the boat was called the *Reef Encounter*. While we were on the boat, they told us there would be a chance to go scuba diving taster. I decided to take them up on that. After the first dive, I was hooked. The amazing colours and sights of fish, coral reef, turtles—it all reinforced my love for God and my thoughts that only he could have created this universe.

We both completed our beginner's diving course, and then I had the little matter of getting my medical done so I could get my diver's card. At first, when we were back in Cairns, I went to a GP practice to have the medical done. However, it was flagged that I had already been refused a diving permit, as this was the same practice where the doctor had been sent from to the PADI course we had initially started. I had to get my medical from somewhere within the Cairns district. We were visiting a friend of Saqib's in Townsville, and this is where I had my medical completed. I barely managed to pass, as on my spirometry, it was found that I had slightly lower lung functioning for my height.

The rest of the holiday went well, and we visited the beautiful Whitsunday Islands and Fraser Island, finishing in Sydney. Throughout this time, I was suffering from lethargy. This included weight gain, the most significant side effect of my treatment. The symptoms took their toll on my holiday, and people would ask why I was sleeping so much. However, I still managed to make the most of the holidays under the circumstances, and it was a turning point for my recovery. After visiting Australia, I remember thinking, if heaven is a place on earth, it's here—from the colours and wonders of the Barrier Reef to the squeaky clean sand on Whitsunday Islands.

I would return from Australia to Manchester, where my wife was there to greet me. Then we made our way back to Sheffield. At this time, because my wife was not aware I had stopped taking my medication while on holiday, I had to reinstate the medication rather than confronting her and admitting what I had done. This would cause a little bit of distance between Liz and me, as I thought I could do without the medication, and she was still under the impression the medication was essential for my wellbeing. I remember I would start to hide the tablets she would give me instead of taking them. On one occasion, we were in Scotland for a short break, and she gave me my medication in the morning, which I hid under the bed. Before leaving the hotel, she must have looked under the bed and found them, which she confronted me about and made me take them.

Our relationship was never the same after the diagnosis, and I recall Liz saying she would leave me, but people would think it was only because of the illness—which does not give a husband confidence in his marriage. You begin to wonder what your relationship is built upon. Anyhow, we carried on living together and making the most of our situation. Then, towards the end of the year 2005, Liz's dad, Alan, had to go into hospital for a heart bypass operation. Although now, I see how much of a strain it must have been on Liz at the time, I resented how much time she would spend in Manchester, where he was having this operation.

This was the point where things seemed to go downhill. Then, in early 2006, I was seen by psychiatrist, and I slowly weaned off my medication. Then, I was formally discharged from the mental health services. What a relief! I felt as though I had conquered bipolar disorder once and for all. By this time, I had started my supplementary prescribing course at Leeds University, which I had started three years previously but had abandoned because of my illness. My life seemed to be back on track. Both Liz and I had started using our treadmill, which had been collecting dust in the garage for many years. As I was not on the medication anymore, the weight started dropping off me. In addition to running, I had started playing football again.

The energy, which had been zapped from me, had come back, and it felt like a complete recovery. Some days, I would even not think about the fact that I had ever been ill, which, for the past two or three years, had been a constant burden on my mind. Nevertheless, I felt I had entered a new era in my life; despite a slight setback, the future looked bright.

I had been in the same job for four years, and things were getting a bit stale at work. I had started looking for the next adventure in my work life. The job in Sheffield was one of the first to have pharmacists working in general practices, but now, I was ready for my next venture. One day, while I was sat in surgery, I was flicking through the pharmaceutical journal, which would advertise all the vacant pharmacy jobs. There was an advert for a pharmacist to work with two GP practices that were opening a new purpose-built health centre in Garstang (which was just north of Preston in the northwest of England).

I proceeded to apply for the job without consulting my Liz. I rang the practice manager and explained my position—that I was working as a practice pharmacist with experience and was also a community pharmacist. I also told them it was not the position of pharmacist I was looking for but rather the role of superintendent pharmacist, with a view towards becoming a partner in the business. Soon, I was called up by Dr Jonathan Williamson, with whom I had a short conversation. Then, I was asked to write in, including my CV and a covering letter.

At this point, I decided to tell Liz I had applied for the job in Garstang. She was not happy at first but soon came round to idea when I explained the prospect of becoming a partner in the practice.

I attended the interview at Garstang, which was with the senior partners, Dr Giles, Dr Mel John and Dr Jonathon Williamson. The interview went very well. Then I made my way back to Sheffield. The next day, I got the call to say they were interested in appointing me as the superintendent pharmacist, with a view towards partnership within a year.

This was followed by the turmoil of relocating to Garstang. At first, Liz was on board and looking forward to it, even though she was a little apprehensive about the move. We started to look for a house in areas surrounding Garstang. We viewed some new builds, which the partners told me to avoid. As we were searching, we came across a barn that was being converted into row houses. We both really liked the development and put in an offer for a three-bedroom barn. At the time, we were still living in Sheffield. Then it dawned on me: for another hundred thousand pounds, we could have a more spacious four-bedroom barn. I quickly consulted Liz, and she reluctantly agreed.

It was now April 2006, and I was due to start work at Garstang Medical Centre. To facilitate my move to Garstang, the doctors had agreed to rent out a two-bedroomed cottage for me in Scorton, a little village just north of the main town in which I would be working. Also, the barn conversion we were looking to buy was in the vicinity of Scorton village. Everything was going well with my mental health. I was full of energy and looking forward to my move to Lancashire. For two weeks, just before cottage was to rent out to me, I moved in with my cousin Sonia, who lived in Ribchester, about twenty minutes away from Garstang. Sonia was a busy solicitor with her own firm, and we were both burning the candle at both ends.

I remember the time I spent with Sonia and her husband, Martin. We would be up early, and then, by eight o'clock in the evening, we would be in the pub down the road, eating fillet steak most nights while enjoying a few drinks. Both Sonia and I were flying high in our careers and felt like we were on cloud nine. One night out in Manchester, at Lowry Hotel, we arrived late for a fashion show; her client had arranged tickets for us, and they had saved us front-row tickets. It could not get much better than this as we sipped malt whiskey with the beautiful models strutting their stuff just a yard away from us.

I was delighted with life once again and feeling invincible. However, I never could have anticipated what happened over the next few weeks. By this time, I had moved into my rented accommodation in Scorton. We had a blip at work one week before our pharmacy was due to open—the health authority refused our one-hundred-hour pharmacy licence. The next thing I knew, we one the phone to solicitors and barristers who were specialists in this field. The partners were commented they would all be willing to put in two hundred thousand pounds each to fight for our right to a pharmacy license.

This pharmacy was no ordinary pharmacy. It was going to be a brilliant pharmacy, and I had input into its design and layout. We had five computer stations for dispensing medication. In both consulting rooms, the pharmacy also had dual desktops with GP practices clinical systems on them. These enabled the pharmacist to consult with patients. At the time, we employed a pharmacist named Helen, who was going to be assistant manager. When we had this hiccup with the pharmacy licence, Jonathan said not to worry; both of us would be employed by the surgeries.

When it came time for the health centre to open, we ended up with a dispensing licence instead of pharmacy licence for all our patients. So, we were allowed to dispense only to patients who lived one mile away from the pharmacy. This meant we could supply medication for only half our registered patients. We had a list size of twenty thousand patients between the two surgeries. This amounted to, according to data from the prescription pricing authority, thirty thousand items per month, which were prescribed by both surgeries. This equated to a turnover from prescriptions alone to three and half million pounds a year. We were getting great deals from drug companies. For example, at the time, we were getting Lipitor tablets (for high cholesterol) at eight pounds and being reimbursed twenty-eight pounds for the privilege of sticking a label on them. You can just imagine the amount of money we would be making from this venture.

So, as far as money was concerned, things were looking very good. I already had three houses and was buying a barn conversion, and my earning potential at the pharmacy was fantastic. It was 2006, and the property-investment scene was booming. Everybody was remortgaging and using equity gained in their properties to buy more property. Property prices were at an all-time high. I had become a capitalist.

At the weekends, Liz and I would get together either in Sheffield or Garstang. Things were all right between us, but not great. I was working from six in the morning to almost eight at night to cope with the demands of the pharmacy. Then, after eight, I would end up in the local pub in Scorton, called The Priory. I would have a bite to eat there and then spend the rest of the night propped up at the bar drinking with locals. I would usually go to bed after midnight and then back up for 5 a.m.

Jonathan had arranged for Liz to be interviewed at a local school for a teaching position. This would be in May. But just before the weekend this was due to happen, Liz came up to Scorton, and my cottage was a mess, to say the least. I just did not have time to get it cleaned. This was the beginning of the end of our relationship.

A couple of weeks after Liz's birthday (25 April), she came to visit me on the weekend in Scorton. We had intended to spend the weekend walking in the countryside. However, when Liz got to the cottage, because of all the time I was working and in the pub, the place was a mess, with clothes all over the place. To say the least, she was not impressed. We ended up arguing over the situation. The argument didn't last very long. We went to bed, not talking, and in the morning, without saying very much to me, Liz left. She had a job interview lined up in Garstang, which she cancelled (or said she would not attend). I took this to mean her intentions were not to move in with me.

At this point, I realized our marriage was over. I remember telling my brother Wasif about the situation, but he did not seem too interested; however, my older brother, Saqib, showed some empathy for my situation. My dreams of moving in to the converted barn were down the drain. The next thing I did was go out looking to buy a Porsche to cheer myself up. I ended up back in Sheffield, where I had test-driven the Cayman S. The waiting list for this car was six months, but I could not wait. There was one that was two months old, in blue, which had been brought back to be sold, but it was two thousand pounds over the list price of a brand-new one.

However, I could not wait that long, so a paid over the odds for the blue Cayman S. This improved my mood, but I should have realized that impulse buys and lack of sleep, which afflicted me, were both signs of bipolar disorder. Liz and I had been in contact with each other, and she said we should both make a list of what we could do to keep our relationship going. I returned to our marital home in Sheffield, but I hadn't written a list. She had one and was annoyed I had not made an effort to produce mine. At the time, I was sick of spending all my spare time with her family and friends, and my only request was to devote equal time to mine. She refused point blankly, as she was used to spending so much time with her people. Therefore, I told her I was not willing to carry on with this relationship and it was over as far as I was concerned.

Full of energy, I ended up going to a barbeque in Cambridge at my cousin Ayyaz's house. We all went into Cambridge city centre, where I concluded that I needed a holiday. So, I went into the flight centre in the city centre and booked a holiday to Japan, Hong Kong, and Australia. During this weekend at Cambridge, my cousin Ziad, who was studying for a PhD, asked me if I would like to come to a high table dinner at Hartford College in Oxford. Nobody had noticed anything peculiar about my behaviour, although reflecting back on the situation, it was about this time that I had started losing touch with reality.

The pharmacy was now open, and I was given quite a lot of locum cover to start off with, which meant I had some free time to be away from the pharmacy. This probably was not good, as I now went looking for somewhere to live. There were two semidetached barn conversions located near a small village called St Michaels, and I ended up putting down a deposit on them. Work was getting busier and more stressful than ever.

CHAPTER 7

THE HIGH TABLE- OXFORD

The weekend came, and it was time to drive down Oxford. I had booked a room at the Randolph Hotel. Ziad picked me up from the hotel, and we went to Hartford College. When we arrived, all the undergraduate students were seated at the lower tables in the hall, while we sat with the professors and other PhD students and guests on a slightly raised stage (the "high table"). We started our meal, and the conversation turned to health service. I began to explain how I used to work for the health authority before putting into practice evidence-based medicine, but now, we had started to work for a GP practice where the emphasis was to rip off the NHS and make as much money as possible. By this time, we had finished our meal, and one of the professors—or dons, as they like to be called—decided we should bring the proceedings to an end.

It was all very nice, and I thought that would be the end of the evening. However, one of the dons led the party of people, who amounted to about fourteen, from the high table up into the room and a long old brown mahogany table in the middle, surrounded by seats. It was a very elegant boardroom. As we entered the room, we were all told where to sit by the don. To my surprise, I was asked to sit in one of the most prominent seats, in the middle. Then we were offered some nice wine by the dons. Soon a discussion took place, including some of the most intelligent people in the country. This did not phase me, as I was on a high and not intimidated by the dons.

The conversation became a little bizarre. One of the dons, who was a mathematician, proceeded to tell us how there were plans to build a tunnel between England and New York. Everyone seemed to take this seriously. I thought, *What a load cod's wallop*. Maybe the don was just testing how far he could take the conversation before anyone objected to his ludicrous ideas. This tunnel would propel pods through a tunnel beneath the Atlantic, using forces created by a vacuum system. Everybody was listening and taking in this farfetched idea. Obviously, the PhD students felt they could not contradict the dons, as they were supervising their studies.

I just had to tell them that the physics to make the three-thousand-mile vacuum propelled tunnel did not seem realistic. They changed the subject to travel. The same don said he liked to lie back and let his *mind* travel. By this time, I'd already had a few glasses of wine, and I proceeded to tell him I like to travel as well, but via jet plane, to other countries, to take in the beauty of the earth and experience other cultures. He seemed to be on a completely different wavelength, referring to travel in the psychedelic sense, perhaps referring to hallucinations. Anyway, because I twice now had the audacity to disagree with the don, they decided to bring the proceedings to an end.

We left Hartford college, and Ziad gave me a lift back to the hotel. He came up to my room and told me he thought I might be relapsing back to symptoms of bipolar disorder. I just ignored him, but I should have taken note, as he was a medically trained doctor. However, as soon as Ziad left, I decided to head down to the hotel bar. There I sat down at a table, next to two gentlemen, and I ordered myself a double whiskey and started chatting to the two men.

The two men quizzed me about what I would like to achieve in life, and I proceeded to tell them I wanted a fairer and more equal world. Also, I wished to reduce inequalities among people in the UK. They answered I should go back to university at Oxford and study PPE. I was unaware what this subject was, a combination of philosophy, politics, and economics. We talked about how I was going through a divorce, and it turned they were both divorced as well. They told me they both taught PPE at Oxford. They said they could help me gain the A levels needed to enrol on the course. What a good starting point that would be, they said, to get into politics and become mayor of Manchester. They also asked, "How gay are you?" In these days, this would help to minister to the diverse community found in the UK.

This conversation got my mind buzzing, and now I was dreaming again. Not only was I thinking I had a special and powerful connection with God, but I was now going to go back to university with the goal of becoming an MP. After being at the high table and having this conversation, I was on cloud nine and thought God was making all this happen and opening doors for me to administer his will on earth, which would bring equality and tranquillity to all his people. I think I enjoyed talking to these two gentlemen more than I did being at the high table. However, overall, the experience of visiting this beautiful historical city was amazing.

The next day, my mind was buzzing. I had a new goal in life, to read PPE at Oxford. Who was I kidding? I had just managed to pass pharmacy, and even though lately, my academic skills had got better, enrolling in the MSc at Aberdeen? I was having all sorts of confusing thoughts and getting carried away with myself. I'd had thoughts of going into politics before but did not know how to get involved and what training I would need. Although there is no definite route into politics, PPE gives a good grounding in the disciplines needed to become an MP, and many of them study this course at university.

I ended up going back to work on Monday, trying to hold things together. The pharmacy was busy, and I still needed somewhere to live. So, in a hyperactive state, I decided to put down a deposit on two barn conversions, which, at the time, I probably could not afford. Later that week, I would venture back to Sheffield for the weekend, but instead of staying at my house, where Liz would also be, I decided to book into a hotel. The hotel I stayed in was the St Paul's Macdonald Hotel. As soon as I booked into the hotel, I went to the bedroom, freshened up, and got ready to go to a leaving do for Bhavana, a colleague in Sheffield.

Before I went to the venue of the leaving do, I decided to have a drink at the hotel bar. While at the bar, the bartender told me to come back to the bar later that evening, as there would be a disco night. I walked down to the restaurant, where all of my friends were. While there, as I was now earning a lot more than my ex-colleagues, and I decided to buy two bottles of champagne. My friends perhaps sensed that my bipolar disorder symptoms were coming back and even made comments saying so. At one point, I asked my colleagues, "Do you know who I am?"

Bruce answered, "The future prime minister."

I do not recall what I said or whether I even answered him, but I remember becoming paranoid. When I asked the question, I was thinking that I was a prophet, but they came back with "prime minister," which felt like too much of a coincidence considering what had happened the previous week at Oxford.

CHAPTER 8

NEW LIZ

I swiftly left the restaurant and returned to the hotel; the time must have been about ten o'clock, and there was no party going on. I sat at the bar and had a drink, then decided this was enough for tonight and headed towards the lifts to go to bed. As I was walking towards the lifts, I noticed two girls who had come into the hotel foyer. I asked if I could buy them a drink, and to my surprise, they said yes. We went to the bar and ordered the drinks, then sat down at one of the tables in the bar area. I started chatting to the one, who was slightly shorter and less attractive, as I thought I had a better chance with her. Then, the more attractive one started chatting to me, and we soon fell into deep conversation, each agreeing that an individual is made up of the experiences they have encountered in their life.

We were both agreeing with each other and getting on like a house on fire. In fact, her friend could not believe what she was seeing and just sat back, relaxed, and kind of smirked at how well we were getting on. Then the conversation got on to how old we were. She proceeded to tell me she was twenty years old, at which point, I did not disclose that I was thirty years old, but they proceeded to tell me I only looked like I was twenty-six to twenty-seven. I asked this beautiful girl what her name was. She answered, "Liz."

I could not believe she had the same name as my wife. In disbelief, I asked her again what her name was, to which she answered, somewhat incredulously, "Liz."

She was so beautiful that she did not understand why I was asking for the second time what her name was.

I had never had such a wonderful conversation with a girl before and felt so happy. This was the beginning of something very special. Then we talked about what Liz was studying at university, and she proceeded to tell me, "English Literature." I had presumed she was studying this, at Sheffield University. By this time, there were just two of in the conversation, and we got on to the topic of how in September, I had booked a holiday to go to Australia and was going to go backpacking down the east coast. She replied that she preferred to stay in five-star hotels.

I bit the bullet and asked Liz if she would like to go out with me for a meal. To my delight, she answered yes. We exchanged numbers. I read out my number to her, and she texted me hers. As I received the text, my whole body shook for a moment. As I saved the number, I deleted my wife's, as they were both called Liz. As Liz was leaving, she asked me if it was OK that she was Catholic. I responded, "Yes, that's fine." Then it dawned to me that I had been separated from my wife, and for us to marry, I would have to divorce from Liz first. Then, I would not be able to marry in a Catholic church. This presented a problem, but really, the problem would be for her, not me. They both left, and as they walked away, I remember looking at Liz. She was wearing a pair of blue jeans and had a perfect bum. As I got up to walk to the elevator, a waiter came over to me and handed me a prawn sandwich. I am sure I had not ordered that, but the waiter reassured me that it was mine.

I was so excited that I could not wait to contact her, so I sent her a text saying, "Conversation and love are the keys to happiness in life," to which she replied, "On my way, Mum." I think she had meant to message her mum.

I went to bed, and I woke up and feeling excited. Before I set off for Manchester, I rang Liz to arrange a date. However, her mother answered the phone, and I panicked a little and asked if Liz was there. A few minutes later, Liz phoned, and we discussed making a date to go out for a meal. As it was the first time, she preferred to bring her friend and for me to bring a friend as well. She also commented she would be studying for upcoming exams and that she would need two weeks before we could go on our date.

After this, I travelled to Manchester to go to a concert with my friends Nik, Megan, Sarah, Johnny, and Chris. I was feeling highly because of my encounter with Liz and because of the high-table meeting at Oxford. I explained to Nik that the night before, I had met another girl called Liz. He told me he already knew, that I had told him, but I could not recall telling him anything about this, either by phone or by message. We all met up that day at Sarah's house and were due to stay there tonight, so I left my briefcase there. We ended up going to the concert, which was a festival in the park. While there, I had the emerging feeling that people could listen to my thoughts. Not that they would answer me verbally, but they would make gestures that I presumed meant they could hear my thoughts. This made me think I was somebody special, like a prophet. However, to be a prophet, one must hear the voice of God and communicate with him. In my case, I wasn't hearing any voices, but things out of the ordinary were happening around me. At one point, as we sat and listened to music in the park, some people around us were smoking marijuana. At one point, somebody suggested I smoke some cannabis and maybe ask other people whether they had any. I refused verbally.

Then Sarah said to me, "Who are you, Jesus?"

"No," I replied.

In my head, I already knew I was not Jesus and Jesus was before me. I only had the inclination I was some sort of prophet and that to make a difference to people, I needed to get into politics.

I must have been acting erratically, because I told the group I was going to leave, but Sarah had informed security that I had bipolar disorder and was ill. So, as I left the venue, I was stopped at the gate and told by security that an ambulance was arriving to take me to the hospital, as I was ill. I had no choice in the matter; otherwise, I knew the police would be involved would be waiting for the ambulance. The ambulance came, and I got inside. I remember talking to the paramedics, telling them I felt fine and that I was a pharmacist. They understood my unwillingness to go to the hospital, as it could affect my career, but they said, "We need to take you away from here. Otherwise, we will call the police."

They would take me as far as the hospital waiting area, and from there, it was up to me whether to wait and be seen or leave.

I managed to make my way home to Heaton Mersey, and there, I caught up with my cousin Sajjad. I explained that my car had been left at Sarah's house and that my briefcase was there and I needed to retrieve it. I had my car key on me and retrieved the car first. Then I tried to get in touch with Sarah and Nik to find out when they would be back so I could retrieve my briefcase. They informed me they had gone out to drinks and wouldn't be back until much later. I rang them a couple of times, wondering when they would be back. Finally, at around 2 a.m., they were back at the house. I walked in and simply asked for my briefcase. I grabbed it and left. Sarah made a comment, but I just ignored it, and Chris said, "Just let him go." After what had happened in Turkey, I again felt I was some sort of prophet, and I thought I had a special place and connection with God.

Because of this notion that people could hear my thoughts, while in the car with Sajjad, travelling to my aunt's house, and I believed my thoughts could be heard not only those in my vicinity but also by those who might be listening to the radio. The events are a blur. When I got to my aunt's house, nobody was in, so Sajjad and I left.

Then later on I got to my aunt's house again, and I don't quite know why I went there, but she was a religious Muslim lady who told people about Islam, and at this point, I was thinking Christianity was the only true religion, and I assume that promoting a different religion was blasphemous. Therefore, I shouted and swore at her, claiming what she was doing was wrong in the eyes of God. Then I got back in my car. I sped away from her house and made my way back to Heaton Mersey.

By now, my thoughts had rapidly spiralled out of control. I was beginning to think I had some sort of supernatural powers, which brought me closer to God than anybody else on earth. My thoughts were racing, and I was unable to tell what facts were real and which were merely in my head. This, in turn, led to the whole situation becoming worse.

I remember feeling elated and paranoid at the same time. I had this notion that people could hear my thought. This makes it very difficult to think properly, and my thoughts quickly spiralled out of control. I was now with Sajjad, back in Heaton Mersey.

The next day, I was due back at work in Garstang, so I drove back to my rented house there. That night, I went round to a work colleague's house and started playing loud music from my car outside her house. The next morning, when I got to work, I was pulled into the doctors' office (Dr Giles and Dr Williamson). They had noticed my behaviour had become erratic and knew that the night before, I had been to a colleague's house, and they were concerned about me. I remember thinking, and by the power of my thought, I said to them, "We are not going to get into heaven like this."

The reaction I got was quite bizarre. Dr Williamson seemed panicked and picked up the phone, and Dr Giles said to him, "No, don't do this." But Dr Williamson proceeded to call one of his colleagues at another practice for me to be seen. It was as though they could hear my thoughts. They arranged an appointment at a nearby medical centre for me to be seen.

When I got there, I waited a long time in the waiting room, continually asking the receptionist when I was to be seen. I was eventually seen by the doctor, who deemed I did not need to be admitted into hospital now.

I got into my car and went for a drive down some country lane in the forest of Boland, which was very close to where I was living in Scorton. While I was driving down one of these single-lane roads, I saw a pheasant flying above my car. Suddenly, it nose-dived, and its neck got wrapped around my car bumper. There was a pheasant hanging from my car. This got me wondering, *Why would this pheasant commit suicide?* My initial thoughts were that it was some sort of sign from God. Then there was the way its neck was wrapped round the bottom of the bumper and its body was hanging down. I went to get my car washed, and before they took it down, I got them to take a picture of me and the car, which I sent to Liz.

By this time, my thoughts were all over the place. I believed people could hear my thoughts, and their body language suggested they were responding to my thoughts. This made everything very stressful. Imagine how you would feel if you thought people could hear all your thoughts. This was a time of great fear but also excitement. I felt closer to God than anyone else on earth. I thought I was a prophet. Although God wasn't talking to me, I felt unusually elated and had the awareness that this world was temporary and that I was here to help people realize that one day, we will all be judged. My main concern was the inequalities around the world, and I believed I needed to do something with my life that would level the playing field for everyone around the world.

Once I got out of the doctor's surgery, I proceeded to make my way back to Garstang Heath Centre and went into the pharmacy. I was agitated and was soon told to leave, as I shouldn't have been there since I was off sick. I went back home, to my cottage. I went next door and sat down, thinking my neighbour could communicate with me telepathically.

Soon enough, the police turned up. They were there to assess me for mania associated with my bipolar disorder. I remained quiet, as I thought people could hear my thoughts. My neighbour spoke on my behalf, saying he was my representative. The police asked for my parents' number and proceeded to phone them. I went outside to where the officer was phoning my parents, and I heard him speaking to my parents.

"Do you know your son is Jesus?" he asked.

I went back inside. Shortly after this, the ambulance arrived, as the police must have asked for me to be assessed. A doctor and social worker arrived, and I was sectioned and sent to Blackpool Hospital's mental health unit.

Inside the unit, I still felt as if people could hear my thoughts, and the staff and other patients seemed to be reacting to them. It's the strangest feeling in the world, thinking people can hear your thoughts. You become super alert that people will judge you based on what you're thinking, and you begin to communicate with people through your thoughts. This, in turn, leads to stress. Just imagine, every thought of yours being heard by everyone, who thereupon judge as you. Also, I was feeling I was some kind of intermediary between the people and God. This itself comes with great responsibility and a feeling of grandeur. This was overwhelming, and I recall thinking I was there to make the world a fairer place for all people. I had it in my head that they needed to give me control of money so I could equally distribute funds to all the people on earth to make the world a fairer and better place.

Having been in hospital before, I was pretty much used to the routine on the ward. It was chaotic, with many patients, but only one stands out now—a young lad in his twenties, who used to claim he had tried to be crucified. Looking back on this, he was seriously ill. Anyway, he took a shine to me, and we became quite friendly. Then he got some leave. He asked me if I needed anything from the shops. Being in my manic bipolar mood, I asked him to get me a pair of Diesel jeans. I still thought I could communicate to people through my thoughts, and he asked for my bank card, which I gave him. Then I told him my PIN via my thoughts. He handed me a card with my card's PIN on the back. The result was that he got me the jeans, but he also ended up taking three thousand pounds out of my account.

At this same time, my wife, Liz, was trying to get in touch, but I kept refusing to talk to her. Then, one day, while I was still on the ward, I accepted her call, and she said she could come up from Sheffield and see me, but I ended up telling her I had found someone else. That was the last time she tried to contact me. It hadn't been the easiest of times for Liz and me due to the distance between us—on top of my new job and the added complication of my relapse.

As you can tell, my mental state was impaired, I was taking decisions that would have a profound effect on my life and that of my wife. All this was done in haste and the fact that I was looking forward to going out with the new Liz, about whom I knew nothing apart from the fact we'd had one amazing conversation and connected as I never had before. Looking back, it was a big gamble, but in my head, this shiny new Liz was a better prospect than staying with my wife, who had stood by me for ten years. Just because of one rift and meeting this young lady, I let my marriage deteriorate. Although, to be fair, we were rocky and had split up before I met new Liz.

I was in hospital for at least four weeks, during which I recall many people hearing my thoughts. Without responding orally, their body language led me to believe this was the situation. Being an inpatient on a mental-health ward is a stressful environment, as patients can be acutely ill and, in turn, be aggressive towards one another, which can be stressful and a little scary.

At some point, I ended up at a jeweller's in Preston and ended up buying a heart-shaped diamond ring for Liz. Then I proceeded back to my digs at Scorton Hall, where I showed this ring to my neighbours. We were in their kitchen, and the ring was in its case on the worktop. The three of us were there, and then suddenly, we were left looking for the ring. It had vanished. All three of us were frantically, looking for this ring, but it seemed to have vanished. Then I went into my part of the house to look for it. The lady said she had found it was on the worktop where we had been looking at it. It was as if magic had occurred—it had disappeared and then returned to the same place. Because of this, I put the ring in the safe in my portion of the house.

CHAPTER 9

ROME

Back to the hospital wards. I do not know if the best thing to do with mentally disturbed patients is to stick them all on one ward. When one's mind is impaired, one may become paranoid due to the odd behaviour of other patients who are suffering from various illnesses. This, in turn, may boil over into conflict and aggression between patients. On the other hand, I do not think it is practical to place mental-health patients on general wards, as other patients may feel at risk and there is the escape risk and safety of others to be considered.

Getting back to the hospital in Blackpool, this was my second admission, and I was soon beginning to understand how to play the game. All the information of people hearing my thoughts and thinking I am closer to God than anyone else were never disclosed to my treating team. I was aware of how bizarre this would sound. Also, my diagnosis implied I would labelled as a schizophrenic, which would make it difficult to remain on the register as a pharmacist.

Slowly but surely, as an inpatient, I would accept the medication they gave me. This time, however, I was determined not to have olanzapine, which at high doses, slows you down and makes you put on tonnes of weight. In the end, the treating team psychiatrist agreed to start me on quetiapine (Seroquel). They didn't mess about with dosing and stuck me straight on a high dose. Anyway, now accepting treatment and getting a little bored with the tediousness of being cooped up in hospital, I determined to get out of this place. So, I became more sedate in nature and began to keep myself to myself. This, in turn, would do the trick, and I would be discharged from hospital.

After discharge from Blackpool Royal, I went back home to stay with my parents for a little while, as the cottage I had had been vacated by my brothers. At the time, my aunty and uncle were over from Lahore. They were planning to go on holiday somewhere in Europe, finally settling on Rome. I was still unwell, not fully recovered. It was difficult to forget all the things that had happened to me. Some may claim it was a miracle; others may say it was mind playing tricks on me. Eventually, the time came for my parents and aunty and uncle to go on holiday.

I decided to take them to the airport in my mum's car. When we got to the airport, as they were flying with Lufthansa, they had a desk at Terminal 1, Manchester Airport. I had brought my passport with me on the off chance I got a ticket. Anyway, the desk checked the availability of flights there and back on the same flights as my family. The staff behind the desk started to laugh and said, "Yes, it is possible," and just like that, I was on my way to Rome, just days after being discharged from hospital.

As soon as we arrived in Rome, I realized I did not have any of my medication, so I went to the local pharmacy and explained I was a pharmacist in England and did not have my bipolar disorder medication with me. I managed to get some of it. That evening, we had dinner. Then I went to the rooftop bar in the hotel to have a couple of drinks. So far, so good. Then I realized the Casio G-shock watch I was wearing started to flash on its own, without me pushing the button for the light. In my mind, this was another miracle. So, I decided to ask God questions, and depending on what he wanted me to do, this would make the watch flash or not. This, in turn, heightened my awareness that I was closer to God than anyone else on earth. To top it off, I was in one of the holiest cities in the world.

I can't remember how much sleep I got that night, but it did not equate to that many hours. The next day, I stayed with the rest of the group, and we visited the Colosseum. It was very impressive.

I knew about Rome's relevance for Catholics. I spoke to some tour guides, who told me about the Vatican tours. I went back to my parents and told them about the tours and their relevance to Catholics. They were not too keen on the idea, probably because they were all Muslim. Also, Rome was renowned for its shopping, and they wanted to visit the shops.

By this time, I was high again, feeling on top of the world. On the other hand, I would be sad and angry with people at the state of the world, and I couldn't understand why, 2,000 years after Jesus was on earth, the entire world didn't believe in God and were not Catholic or Christians.

I went on a private tour of the Sistine Chapel. There was a meeting point. When I got there, I started talking to two girls from Ireland who were Catholic. They seemed nice, and we exchanged small talk. We went into the chapel, and it was stunning—beautiful high ceilings with glorious pictures depicting scenes from the New Testament. As I was looking at the pictures, it occurred to me that most of the pictures were of Jesus as he was going to be crucified. In each picture, he had next to nothing on. This started me thinking how disgraced Jesus must have felt in his final hours. I became angry. I remember talking to God in my thoughts, saying what a disgrace it was how he had been depicted in the pictures.

Then, inside the chapel, was a gift shop. I noticed a set of his-and-hers gold crosses, so I bought them for Liz and me. Then I put the velvet case they came in my pocket with the crosses in the case. I roamed around Rome, going into the churches, begging for God to send Jesus back to sort out the mess of the world.

I made it back to the hotel and remember asking my mum and dad for more money, which they were reluctant to give me. So, I went to my aunty, and she gave me some. I went to hotel's rooftop bar and ordered a pint. While I was drinking the pint, my dad asked what I was doing, and I said I was going out. Then I proceeded to run out of the hotel, and he followed me. As I turned the corner, I thought I heard him fall. I went back round the corner, and he wasn't there. Then I had my phone in my hand, and suddenly, I thought everyone in my contacts was a waste of time and proceeded to throw the phone in the bin.

Suddenly, I found myself in a shoe shop, trying on new shoes. But when it came time to pay, something went wrong with the payment, and I found myself walking around in Rome, near the Vatican, with bare feet. I remember being disorientated, unable to find my way back to the hotel.

What happens next is probably the most memorable scenario of my life. I was walking barefoot around Rome, accompanied by my thoughts of grandeur. Suddenly, I felt as if I were being tested by God. My main objective was to get back to the hotel in one piece. Then I looked up to the night sky, and it was full of stars. Then, the most amazing thing happened. One by one, each star flashed, then went out. This happened very quickly. Then all the stars flashed at once, and the sky was lit up. It was like the most powerful flash you can imagine going off and experiencing the most amazing brightness amid the darkness. Then, without any clouds in the sky, it started to rain—just a slight drizzle.

At the time, I was wearing my glasses, and suddenly, while wearing them, my eyesight became a bit blurry. I took off the glasses, and my eyesight was better than ever. I could see everything clearly—everything was sharp, as if I had been wearing glasses. At the time, my prescription was -4.00 in both eyes, so without glasses, I could hardly see anything. Now, however, my eyesight was perfect. I knew this might be temporary, so I kept hold of my glasses. By this time, I was absolutely starving, and I remember eating a leaf, which was horrible. Also, I drank water from a fountain.

I couldn't tell if other people had seen what I had, but I felt euphoric, on top of the world. It was as if the flashing stars were an acknowledgement from God.

Around this point, I checked my pockets for the crosses that I had bought. To my surprise, the pouch was there, but the crosses weren't. I searched every pocket for them but simply couldn't find them. Then, as I was walking around, I felt a little tapping sensation in my pocket. I took out the pouch, and the crosses were back in it.

I looked down at my feet; they had become dirty and had a couple of cuts. I remembered from my pharmacy training that urine was sterile, so I proceeded to urinate on my feet. Then I thought I really needed to get back to the hotel. I was absolutely starving. However, I only had an underground ticket, and it was closed at this time in the morning. Then, suddenly, the light returned to the sky, and morning was here. The underground opened, and quite a few people were waiting to get back home. Then they started to close the entrance to the underground again.

I had to find an alternative way home. I suddenly realized that the buses were starting to run again. As I was waiting for a bus, I noticed a pizza shop open. I went in and explained I had no money. They must have noticed I had been through the mill, as the man behind the counter gave me a small pepperoni pizza. It was a lifeline. Then I approached a bus with my train ticket, and the driver just let me on. I got off at the main bus stop, which was near the central train station, where our hotel was.

When I got back to my room, it had been vacated, so I went to my parents' room. They told me they had reported me missing to the police. By now, I was very tired, so I got some rest. I did not get good sleep, unable to believe what had happened to me. Obviously, my parents were very worried, saying I had been gone the better part of two days.

In the morning, I had to borrow shoes from my dad. It was a three-night stay, and I had stayed in the hotel for only one night. We organized a taxi from the hotel to the airport, as we were leaving this morning. The taxi was bizarre; it was as if the driver didn't know where he was going. We got to the airport, and all the flights going out seemed to be delayed. When we got to Frankfurt, we were taken straight off the flight and took a straight to our connecting flight to Manchester. On this flight, I had a couple of drinks. Again, I felt as though everyone could hear my thoughts. In addition, the flight attendants were acting peculiar, wearing watches on both arms and waving their arms around. I remember this young girl sitting in the aisle next to me. She was wearing Swiss K shoes. As I was looking, her nose seemed to change sizes. I was obviously having some sort of hallucination.

By the time we landed in Manchester I was again acutely ill. I remember getting my bag and running through immigration. I was following this girl, who at the time I thought I knew. Then she said to me, "Are you following me?" I said no. Then I got out into the arrivals area, and I must have been acting bizarrely. My mum's friend was there to greet us and take us back home. I proceeded to the airport shop and tried to buy some cigarettes. The next thing I knew, security was there. I being questioned by airport police. I seemed to be able to talk to them without speaking, and the officer responded to me by ripping off his Velcro badge, which said, "Police" on it.

Then the inevitable happened: I was being taken to Stepping Hill Hospital to the psychiatric unit. When I got there, they had put me in the secure unit. My God, there were some scary people in there. I remember complaining when one of the other patients grabbed me by the neck and began to strangle me. But there was no use. This sort of thing happened on these wards, all the time.

I spent a few days on this ward before I was ferried off to Preston Hospital. The taxi to the hospital took next to no time. It felt as if just as I got into the cab, we were on the motorway, and the next thing, we were there.

I had the biggest shock when I got there. I was put in solitary confinement, locked up in my cell most of the day. It was one of the most horrific experiences of my life. There was nothing to do, and I received visitors only a couple of times a week. This was a depressing time. I was allowed out to watch TV for one hour a day, and even the TV would not work properly. After a couple of weeks on this ward, I was transferred to the low-security ward. Luckily, the doctor on this ward thought I was well enough to be discharged, and I just stayed in a couple of nights more.

When I was discharged, I moved back to Heaton Mersey. I was living with my brother Wasif, round the corner from my parents. By this time, it was the end of August, and at the beginning of September, I had a holiday booked to Australia, Tokyo, and Hong Kong. Even though I had just come out of hospital, I decided I was well enough to go travelling on my own. I was contacted Liz one day when I was in Sheffield, but she was unable to meet that day. I told her I would be going on my trip, and she said, "Take care of yourself."

The day came for me to travel. I got to the airport, but the travel agents, Flight Centre Cambridge, had messed up the flights. I was supposed to be travelling to Tokyo, but my flight from Manchester was to Hong Kong. I kept my cool, and the man behind the check-in counter helped me get in touch with the travel agent. He remarked that I was very calm considering the situation. Little did he know that I had bipolar disorder and that if I started to cause a scene, the only place I would be going was hospital. As I recall, they told me to board the flight to Hong Kong, and when I got there, they would have something sorted out for me.

So, the only option I had was to go to Hong Kong. I got to Hong Kong Airport, and they had arranged for me to stay at the Airport hotel and then catch the next flight out to Tokyo. So, I ended up spending no significant time in Hong Kong and one day less in Tokyo. In Tokyo, I was staying at the Park Hyatt Hotel. This hotel was fantastic, with great facilities. The toilet even gave your bum a wash and dry. I went to the hotel bar each night, where I paid ten pounds for a pint, and there was an extra charge of ten pounds for the live pianist. Tokyo was nice—lots of technology and sushi.

The next day, I flew into Cairns. I had booked accommodation for one night here. I arrived at my backpacker's hostel. Everything seemed to be fine for the time being. I enjoyed drinks with the other residents and even had the budget spaghetti Bolognese for my tea. After staying there for one night, I asked if could extend my stay for another couple of nights, to which they agreed. This is where the trouble started. I remember going out in central Cairns and drinking. My situation taking the tablets had gone downhill again.

I was due out on the reef encounter, which was the same boat we had gone on when I was there with my brothers. While there, I signed up for a diving refresher course and some dives. My enthusiasm for the dives soon ran out, and I would become more obsessed with drinking. As I was drinking, all sorts of things were going through my head. I was starting to lose control of reality. I remember one day, lying there, looking up in my bunk bed, and I was hallucinating. I could see cartoon characters floating around just above my eyes. It was very soothing.

I knew this was not merely the result of my medication, so I decided to take a dose, but by this time, I was too far down the line in delusions. I had got friendly with one chap, and he started to keep his distance from me. I asked why, and he said, "You are acting peculiar." This reinforced to me that I had to take my tablets. By now, I thought people could hear my thoughts again. Then I remember vividly: I went over to one man who was was sitting with his wife and took his cap off, and his hair started to turn white. This reinforced in my dodgy mind that miracles can happen and that I was central to all this. I was thinking again that I was special to God, more in touch with him than anyone else on earth. The next day, we were due to go back to the mainland. On the way back, the engine of the boat broke down, and we had to wait for a rescue boat. For some reason, I started to throw Australian dollars overboard. People were looking and probably thought I had lost my mind (which I had).

We landed back on dry land, and I had to find somewhere to stay, so I went and checked in to Gilligan's Backpackers, which was in central Cairns. Here I stayed in a shared room. I made friends with another lad in the room, and we decided we go out for drinks, but by now, I was well away with the fairies. I ended up getting drunk, then thinking I would like to stay in Australia, so I ended up tearing up my passport and throwing it on the street. The next thing I knew, I was in a police cell. There were two of us in the same cell. In the morning, we went for a shower. When I came back into my cell, my cellmate had yet to return. Then the door locked, and from nowhere, he appeared. This was crazy. It was as if he had been teleported back into the cell. The police had me assessed by mental health and said I was free to go.

However, the next night, things got bizarre again. I ended up tipping the backpackers 400 dollars just because it said that was the fine for underage, so I thought I had to pay the fine for them. I was crossing a main road and walked up to a tree in an island in the road, and the bark of the tree started changing pattern. At some point after this, I was picked up by police. This did not end well for me, as the next day, I was admitted to hospital in Cairns.

Here, they had realized I hadn't been taking my medication, so they started to titrate my dose back up to 800 mg daily of quetiapine. I remember getting a phone call from one of the doctors from work, saying I needed to come back. This was easier said than done at the time. I was under a section and was on the other side of the world. It took two or three weeks to get my medication back on even keel. While I was in hospital, it turned out I had been charged by the police for breaching the peace. So, while I was there, they had to get me legal help to go to court. At court, the solicitor pleaded I was ill at the time of the accident and asked me to submit a guilty plea. I ended up just getting a fine. By now, my money was running out, and my credit cards had stopped working. One was with American Express and the other with Morgan Stanley.

The mental health ward in Cairns was nice. We used to go swimming once a week, and on Wednesdays, we used to have barbeque for lunch. Soon enough, I started to get bits of leave. I would use this to go and look round the shops. Then, one day, I got a little bit longer out. I used this to go out for a drink—without any money. I got to a bar and put my credit card behind the counter. I remember offering people drinks. Then, at the end of the night, the card bounced. The bar staff were not too happy with this, as I had run up a bill which at the time was about eighty pounds. However, they had no choice but to let me go. To my surprise, when I got back to the ward, I had to have a breathalyzer test for alcohol. As a result, they reduced my leave.

The next thing was organizing a new ticket for me to go home. Luckily, I had flown with Qantas, and the hospital staff managed to get me a replacement ticket from Cairns to London, as my flight had been from Brisbane to Hong Kong for three days, then to Manchester. However, the airline would not let me fly on my own; they needed me to travel with somebody who would supervise my medication. This sparked a whole number of new problems. I was in touch with the mental health team back home. They were not too happy about this, and the cost would be astronomical. The Australians said they would charge something like ten thousand US dollars for a nurse to accompany me back to the UK. Also, while I was using my cell phone to call England, I could put in my parents' phone number without an international code, and it would connect, but it was only their number it would do this for. For every other number I would call in the UK, I would need an international code.

Looking at all the options, my father agreed he would come over to Australia and fly back with me. While I was in the Cairns hospital, I tried to get in touch with Liz a few times, but due to the difference in time, it was difficult. Finally, I got through, and she answered the phone. Because I was calling from Australia, I asked if she knew who it was. She replied, "Of course I do!" I asked her what she was doing. She said, "Lectures and stuff." Then she asked me if I was OK, to which I replied yes. What a lie that was! Ever since I had met her, my life had been turned upside down. Everything was wrong!

My dad ended up come from Manchester to Cairns. He stayed at a hotel opposite the hospital, and that night, he only had time to take a brief taxi ride down to the coast. He had travelled all the way just for one night. He accompanied me in the ward the day that he got there, and then, in the evening, we had dinner with a bottle of champagne. The next day, we boarded our flight back. The Qantas flight was near enough empty. It had two stops—one in Darwin and the other in Singapore.

We got to London, and my mum came to pick us up. Soon enough, we were back in Manchester. However, even though I was taking the medication, my head was still not in the right place. Because of all the hallucinations and miracles I had seen, it was difficult to know what or who I was. Was I just someone who was ill, or had God looked on me favourably, showing me his strength via miracles?

As I was at home, in Stockport, soon enough, my compliance with medication became irregular again. I remember arguing with my parents about religion, and I could not understand why they remained Muslims when all the evidence was telling me Christianity was the real religion. Then, one day, I was in the living room, and they had a crystal model of the Mecca Mosque. Suddenly, I picked it up and said, "This is bullshit," and threw the model at wall, smashing it to pieces. I proceeded to run away from their house and went to a local hotel, where I stayed the night.

Then the next day, I got in my Porsche and drove first to Leeds. Then, as I was travelling down to Sheffield on the motorway, I saw the moon. Then the moon moved to right, so I steered the car to the right, following it, then to the left, and steering the car in that direction. Then the moon did a loop round my car and seemed to disappear. This seemed like a miracle, although reflecting on it now, I was hallucinating. This could not have been real. But to a mind already confused, this sort of thing just made my things worse. Then I was driving home from Sheffield to Manchester, and suddenly, I realized I was low on fuel. I thought I was not going to make it. I looked at the petrol gauge, and the car seemed to have refuelled itself. From being at position where I had nearly run out it was over a quarter full. For me, this seemed like another miracle—the car refuelling itself. However, the weather got bad, and I was on the A roads between Sheffield and Stockport. Visibility was atrocious, and I could hardly see 30 metres in front of me. Then, suddenly, I was Chatsworth House.

As I got to Chatsworth House, I told the person on security I knew the queen and to let me in. He explained that this house belonged to the duke of Devonshire. I asked if there was anywhere I could park and get some rest. The guard told me there was a car park a few hundred metres down the drive. I parked there and tried to get some shut-eye. Then there was a knock on the window. It was the police, informing me I was not welcome to stay there and I should drive away. Then I explained I had tried to drive but couldn't in such poor visibility conditions.

Then next thing I knew, I was getting carted off to hospital in the back of a police car. I stayed one night at the local hospital near Bakewell and was then transferred to Chesterfield Royal the next day. It was the same old thing: they realized I was not taking my medication and started to reintroduce it. By now, it October or November. It had been about six months since I had met Liz, and we still hadn't had a date. So, I got on the hospital payphone and dialled her number. There was no answer at first. Then the phone started ringing. I picked up the phone, and it was Liz ringing back. She asked me, "Are you in Chesterfield Hospital then?"

I answered, "See you on the other side!" then slammed the phone down.

I do not think she was too impressed by this. The next communication I got from her was a text message not to contact her or she would change her number. Then I thought I had better come clean and text her, explaining that I had been diagnosed with bipolar disorder and asked if I could call her. She simply replied, "No." This would be the last time I would hear from Liz.

CHAPTER 10

THE DEPOT

Soon, I would be on the medication again and fooling the doctors that I was all right. Then, if I showed no signs of mania, they had no reason to keep me in hospital. At first, they gave me time off the ward, which I used to go to the cinema and wander round Chesterfield town centre. Then the time came for my discharge. I went back to Stockport. As soon as I got there, I started to have conflicts with my family. This was getting all too tedious—all because I had abandoned their religion and become a follower of Christ. Soon, they were looking for me to slip up. My compliance with the medication became erratic, and I soon found myself trapped in my parents' house. My brother Saqib had trapped me in the back room and would not let me leave. In the meantime, he had called the emergency services, and an ambulance appeared.

This time, my parents insisted I put on a depot injection. I was not happy with this, but in the end, I succumbed, as they would not let me out of hospital without one. This would be the end of the mania once and for all. I remember I was put on zuclopenthixol. I had a test dose, and at first, I got a bit of lockjaw, but this soon abated. I stayed in hospital for about three months.

I got back home to my brother's house. This was now home. It was the beginning of what would be a massive depression. I was questioning everything. Why me? Why did I have to get bipolar disorder? My life before this awful illness had been going fine. I had a good job, a nice wife, a house, and a flat. Suddenly, I was being told not to worry, and my dad asked me, "Why are you so depressed?" It nearly brought me to tears. How could I explain to him everything I had lost to this terrible illness? I had lost my house and wife. And to top things off, this would be the start of the terrible struggle to keep my registration as a pharmacist. Dr Williamson had notified the Pharmaceutical Society I had been ill. Therefore, they had me suspended from the register. No work, no money, no life. From being able to afford a good living with three holidays abroad each year to being stuck in a rut of sleep and boredom.

The medication had slowed me right down, and because of my sedentary lifestyle, I began to pile on the weight. At one point, I went from 32-inch jeans to a 38-inch waistline. I was unrecognizable. This added to my depression. There was no amount of medication that could sort out my depression. How could anyone feel good in this predicament?

Soon enough, I was put back on to fluoxetine. To be honest, I don't think my depression was a mere chemical imbalance; it was circumstantial. I took the fluoxetine for two months before I realized it was not doing any good and I stopped. At one point, I was on 40 mg fluoxetine. I honestly do not know how I got through this time.

I had no money, not even enough to go the local and have the occasional pint. However, my parents had been incredibly supportive when it came to finances. My father would pay the instalments on my car, but otherwise, I was in no man's land. I couldn't claim benefits because I still had my flat, which was rented out. During this time, I remember praying for my life to end. This was the lowest point I had ever experienced. The fate of mental health was one worse than cancer, I thought. At least with cancer, there is a way out. You die and hopefully, go to heaven.

During this time, the one thing that didn't leave me was my faith. I had started to go to the local church, which was the Church of England (C of E). I thought the Catholics wouldn't accept me because I was divorced and therefore unable to take Communion there. However, I never told my parents I would be attending church. Around this time, in 2007, I was baptized in C of E. They would ask me where I had been on a Sunday morning, knowing full well that churches were open at that time, and I would have to lie and say, "Just for a walk."

CHAPTER 11

DEPRESSION AND THE PHARMACUETICAL SOCIETY

During the height of my depression, some days, I would be awake only two hours a day. I was hibernating. I could not see a way out of this awful situation. Until now, I had led a life where time was sparse. I would work six days each week, sometimes over sixty hours in total. The one reason I did not commit suicide was that maybe I didn't have the bottle, or maybe because it was against my religion as a Christian, or perhaps that was a holdover belief from Islam. I had been suspended by pharmaceutical society, meaning I had no means to earn money. Pharmacy was all I had ever known.

After a few months, around May 2007, I began looking for another job, whatever I could get. I ended up in a call centre job for AA, the automobile recovery company. It was all target-driven sales. My experience was that of the worst work environment of my life. Basically, it bored the backside off me. I lasted only three months in this job.

Then I had my review at the Royal Pharmaceutical Society, in Lambeth, London. This was like a day at court. You had to go before a panel with a judge. There was a clinical advisor and solicitor from the society. It was all very daunting. They would assess whether I was fit to work. In the end, they decided my fitness to work was impaired, but I would be allowed to work under certain conditions. These were very severe. I was only allowed to work Monday to Friday, I was not allowed to locum or be a superintendent pharmacist or responsible pharmacist. Also, I had to follow any instructions provided by the mental health team.

Finding a job with these conditions would be very difficult. However, I was adamant I would work in a pharmacy. I began to contact all the pharmacy multiples, as the easiest way back in would be community pharmacy. During Easter 2008, Lloyds pharmacy gave me a job as a relief pharmacist. I was contracted Monday to Friday, and at first, I would just go around to different pharmacies, filling in when the pharmacist manager was off. I found this very tedious. Then, my life as a pharmacist took a turn for the worse: I was given the task of checking nursing-home prescriptions at the Oldham branch. This was very tedious work, checking medication trays for nine hours a day.

By this time, I had put on lots of weight because of the medication and the sedentary lifestyle. My self-esteem was at the lowest point it had ever been. Then I got my driving licence back, which had been revoked due to health reasons. This gave me a little freedom. I also started going to the gym. I had accrued some holidays, so I decided I would take a trip to the land of Jesus, Israel. So, I booked a guided tour for nine days in Israel.

This would be one of the best holidays of my life. The weather was perfect. However, on my entry to Israel, it was a bit tricky. I got there on my flight, and as soon as I got to immigration, they pulled me aside. *Great!* I thought. I had spent all this money, and they were immediately passing judgement. My passport name is Mohammad Atif Yousaf, a proper Muslim name. They asked me all sorts of questions: Why I had come here? Why I had changed religions? Why was I visiting Pakistan? They had put me on the spot, and under the pressure, I could not think. I endured the humiliation of being strip-searched, down to my underwear.

I contacted the British embassy and explained my predicament at the airport. The person at the embassy said, "Just see what happens. If they do not let you in, give us a call back." Finally, after about five hours waiting in the airport, they gave me a three-month tourist visa. They do not stamp your passport in Israel but give you a credit-card sized photo visa. By the time I got out of the airport, the person from the tour company had left the airport. I managed to contact him, and he told me to get a taxi to my hotel in Tel-Aviv.

Tel-Aviv was lovely, with lots of big beachfront hotels. I spent the day walking around. When I went to the shopping mall, there was armed security there. It was a bit of culture shock to me, seeing all this security. But it was all necessary because of the trouble with the Palestinians. The next day, my tour guide came to pick us up in his van. In our group, there were about eight of us, mostly men. Except for myself and one Canadian, the group was all Americans. It was the first time in the Holy Land for all, and the trip did not disappoint.

We went from Tel-Aviv to the ancient city of Caesarea and explored the ruins in the 2,000-year-old city. Then we travelled inland to spend a night at a kibbutz. This was fascinating. I was impressed at how people lived and how they invoked principles of equality. Each person worked at his or her profession—be it lawyer, dentist, cleaner, or any other number of jobs—then all the money went into the pot and was meted out according to the needs of each family. For example, a four-person family would get a three-bedroom house and a certain amount of money, while a three-person family would get a two-bedroom house and an amount of money that met their needs.

One of the ladies talking with us shared her experience of how, when she first came to the kibbutz, despite being a qualified teacher, she was made to work in the dining hall. This way, she got to know all the families. Then, after a couple of years, she went back to teaching. They also had pool cars, which families used when they needed transport. They also told us about one incident in which one of their community residents became ill, and they had the patient flown to Switzerland for the best doctor for that complaint. This way of living was surely the fairest way of treating people, and I was very impressed. Also, if a family suddenly decided they no longer wanted to live in the kibbutz, depending on how long they had lived there, they would get a payout to help them adjust to life outside the kibbutz. This, surely, was the way Jesus would want us to live; after all, it was the Jews who had come up with this fantastic system.

Then the next day, we moved on to Nazareth. This was where Jesus spent most of his life and had grown up. Here, we visited the Church of Annunciation and the basilica. Then we moved on to the Sea of Galilee. This is where Jesus walked on water. We also went to other Christian and Jewish holy sites; the whole experience was very moving.

On the tour group, three out of the eight of us suffered from bipolar disorder. Although this was a coincidence, it made me consider whether there is a link between the illness and spirituality.

Then we spent three days in the most amazing city in the world, Jerusalem. This place was magical. Here lived Jews, Christians and Muslims all in one city. However, they did all live in their specified neighbourhoods.

The place I found the most spiritual was the Wailing Wall. This is where Jesus would have come to pray at the Temple on the temple mount. For some reason, you just get a real sense of near to God when in Jerusalem. We visited all the main sites, including the garden tomb of Jesus. The one place we missed because got there too late was the dome of the rock, Al-Aqsa Mosque.

While in Jerusalem, we visited Bethlehem. This city is now under Muslim control. The whole experience was a little surreal compared to slickness of Tel-Aviv. Here the emphasis was on us briefly visiting the church where Mary gave birth to Jesus. Then we spent a good hour with the new guide, as our usual guide was Jewish and not allowed across the border, purchasing Gifts and souvenirs. I bought a necklace for myself which was made from gold. It was a Star of David with a cross in the middle. Also, I bought a Jerusalem cross.

Soon it would be time to go home, and I had an early morning flight. My taxi came to the hotel on time, and we would leave for the airport. While on the motorway from Jerusalem to Ben Gurion airport, my taxi was stopped by the police. The police officer asked to see my passport, I showed him. Then then taxi driver got back into the car and explained for the many years he had been working taking people to the airport he had never been pulled over. He also explained that he had not been speeding and he thought that it was because of me.

Back in England, around March 2009, I was put in charge of a branch in Stockport. This was much better. I was seeing customers again, and the day was far more interesting. After three months, I was given my own branch in Stockport. It was a small branch with about four staff. It was a good team, and everyone seemed to get on well. However, after a few months, I started to get bored, as it was not much of a challenge and I wanted to pursue a career that was more clinical.

Pakistan- The arranged marraige

In the October of 2009, I landed a job with Christie Hospital, a leading hospital in the country for cancer services. So, I handed in my notice to Lloyds and worked my two months' notice. At the beginning of December, my parents were going to Pakistan for a holiday. They asked me also come along before I started my new job. I had the month of November and some of December off, about five weeks in total. By now, my parents were putting pressure on me to get married again. They were under the impression I had tried my own way by marrying an English girl, which had not worked out, so now I should give an arranged marriage a try with a girl from Pakistan.

I explained my low self-esteem due to my weight gain and divorce. Then, a couple of days before I was to fly out to Pakistan, my mother rang and said she had met a lovely girl and wanted me to meet her. No sooner had I landed in Pakistan before, the next thing I knew, I was in Faisalabad, where my uncle lived, visiting this young girl's house. I was thirty-four at the time, and this girl was just about turning twenty-one or twenty-two. It was one of the most nerve-racking scenarios I had ever experienced. I met the girl with her parents, along with my mum and uncle. Then I had what seemed five to ten minutes alone with her to talk before I had to decide whether or not to marry her. She was a good-looking girl and under pressure to say yes, so I said I would marry her. Two days into a holiday, I was engaged.

The next three weeks were spent preparing for the wedding. For some reason, everything was being done at a hundred miles an hour. The wedding date was set for one week before I left for England. Everything was happening so fast, I hardly had any time to think of the implications. This was a *marriage* I was getting into. The next thing you know, a three-day wedding had been arranged. I was a Christian getting married to a

Muslim in a Muslim country. This was the stupidest thing a person could do. I talked to the girl, Beenish, and she did not seem to be too religious. So, I thought this might work out.

Looking back, I ask myself, *What was I doing?* One minute, I'm on a Christian pilgrimage in Israel. The next, I'm getting about to marry a Muslim girl. Then before I know it, preparations are being made for the wedding. My mother was in her element, shopping for her new daughter in law. Jewellery and clothes are where most of the money went—not to mention a wedding with more than three hundred guests. I knew only about forty of them well enough that I might invite them on my own. The rest were from the other side and my mum and dad's family and friends. My brother Wahib had already been with us, and my brother Wasif flew in from England for the wedding.

The night before the wedding my uncle Sadiq, my dad's older brother, and my dad sat me down and said, "It's not too late if you want to back out." Easy for them to say after the preparations my mother had made. The wedding took place over three days. The first day, in the evening, was the *mendi*, a more relaxed occasion featuring an evening of music. Despite the relaxed mood, my nerves were starting to kick in.

The next day was the wedding day. I got dressed up in the traditional Pakistani groom's attire. From my uncle's house to the wedding venue, I rode on a horse and cart. When we got to the venue, and I sat on the stage at the front. Then the imam came, and the proceedings began—some in Urdu, which I understood, and some in Arabic. All this time, the bride was in another room. They asked her one simple question: whether she agreed or not.

After a fifteen-minute ceremony, I was married once again. There was a lot of hand-shaking and hugging with family. Then the bride came through, and there were endless photographs. After the meal, we went back to my uncle's house, where presents were presented to the bride. The bride and I were then dropped off at the hotel where we would be staying for the next few days. Now, this was the most nerve-racking thing. I was supposed consummate the marriage with a girl I hardly even knew, stone cold sober. Anyway, the deed was done, although it was awkward for both parties. Afterwards, we started to get to know each other and spent most of the night chatting.

The next morning, we had to be at the third part of the wedding, the *walima*. We ended up getting up late, and she had to at the beauticians. So, I threw on a suit, and I didn't even get the chance to iron my shirt. Anyhow, after a lot more photos and a lovely meal, we went back to my uncle's house. Later, back at the hotel, we were in bed, just chatting, and Beenish started asking questions about my history. For example, how I had got to the age of thirty-four and still had not been married. I explained that I had been married before. This went over like a lead balloon. She started crying and saying she had not been informed about this. *Great*, I thought, *another marriage down the drain*. She had stopped talking to me.

I called my mother to come and see us and sort out the situation. My mother came, and she was adamant that her parents had been told about my previous marriage to an English girl. The next day, we were due to travel about four hours away to my cousin's wedding. However, because of what had happened, she was reluctant to go. So, the rest of the family went while we were left behind. Then after a couple days, she calmed down and got used to the idea of my previous marriage. We made it to the third day of my cousin's wedding.

Following this, we had three days in Lahore, at my aunty's house. Here, we got to know each other a little better, but soon it was time to go home. One minute I was married, the next, back in England alone again. Beenish and I talked every day on the phone. She was in her final year university, so she could not come to England until she had finished. In the meantime, I had applied for her visa.

Back at home in Manchester, I had started my new job at Christie hospital. The team here was a young one. I made new friends, and the social scene was good. Most of the pharmacists in the department were girls. We had lots of nights out. Then, in March, I booked off three weeks to go to Pakistan to meet up with my wife. Time seemed to be flying by, and I was once again enjoying life.

Since we'd had such a rushed wedding, without much time to spend together, we decided to go on a honeymoon. Beenish did not have a passport yet, so we were limited as to where we could go. But in the end, we decided to go to Skardu. We stayed at a resort on Shangrila lake. We were there only four days. From our resort, there were many excursions, which took us to all the nearby attractions. We took a trip to look at the peak of K2 and also a boat trip on Lake Satpara. It was the most idyllic place to spend our honeymoon. In the evenings, I wanted to spend time in a restaurant, while Beenish was more interested in staying in the room and watching TV. One night, I actually went for dinner on my own. On our way back, we got to the airport, and while waiting for our flight back to Islamabad, we were informed it had been cancelled because of low clouds, meaning the incoming flight could not land. She was not happy about this and went into a bit of a strop. Then next day, we managed to get a flight back to Islamabad.

The holiday was over quickly, and soon, I was back in Manchester. I was back at work and enjoying both the work as a clinical pharmacist and the nights out with my fellow colleagues. Then, after a night out in Manchester, I ended up back at a friend's apartment. The next morning, I explained to Christina that this was not going anywhere, as I was married. I went home feeling guilty. By this time, Christina had left Christie Hospital, so we just stayed in touch outside work.

I decided to end my marriage with Beenish, which did not go down well with my parents. Beenish kept phoning me, and I Was ignoring her calls. The whole thing was one big mess. Then the next thing I knew, Christina wanted to know what I was doing about Beenish, whether I was divorcing her or not. So, under pressure from Christina, I decided to cancel Beenish's visa to the UK. I wrote a letter to British immigration and told them I had been forced into the marriage in Pakistan and to cancel the visa.

My parents were absolutely disgusted at my behaviour. By now, I was living in an apartment in the same complex as Christina. One Friday afternoon, Emer and I had a few drinks after work. When I got back to the apartment, Christina wanted to go out for drinks, so we headed out to a bar in Manchester.

At the bar, everything was going well until Christina went the toilet. When she came back, she said to me, "I saw you looking at them girls!" That was it.

"Just wait here a minute," I said, but she just walked out the door and got a taxi home. That was the end of that relationship. At this point, I wondered whether to try with Beenish again. She was still trying to get hold of me and in touch with my parents. But I decided against it.

I had been taken off my depot medication with the approval of my psychiatrist. They had given me oral medication, but my compliance was not great. With everything that was going on at home with the marriage, everyone thought I was ill. September came, and I had two weeks booked off. Initially, these were to go on holiday with Christina, but as we had split up, I decided to go on holiday with a friend from my local pub in Heaton Mersey, Stockport.

CHAPTER 12

THAILAND

This holiday was Patong, Thailand. I knew exactly what went on in Thailand and, having no partner at time, was looking forward to it. This pace was crazy beyond my wildest dreams. For the first week, I dabbled in the local delicacies. Then I began to find out more about why these girls were in the sex trade—because they did not have many other options. One girl told me they liked to stay over so they could get some proper sleep; otherwise, they were forced to stay in very cramped rooms with girls who were also in the game. I saw husbands drop off their wives, who would then go out and prostitute themselves.

This was a reality check, and I stopped indulging in this unfair practice, using these poor girls. However, I started to drink more and more. With no medication and plenty of alcohol on board, I ended up falling out with Neil and his family, with whom I had gone on holiday. Drunk, I would mouth off to the local Thai men that they were not real men because they let their wives be used as prostitutes. One night, a Thai man punched me in the face, landing on my chin. It seemed as if my chin was dislodged and broken. I put my hand on the side of my face, and as I touched it, the injury seemed to heal itself. I was like another miracle! This gave me the notion I was again closer to God. It's difficult to remember exactly what happened, but I ended up taking a shower, and I stood under the water a long time. Then I remember thinking of Liz, whom I had met in the hotel in Sheffield. Then, in a hallucination, I saw hotel owner's face. I was convinced his face was that of the devil. The next thing I knew, I was standing buck naked in my room with Thai police pointing guns at me. I shouted at them, "Jesus will kill you!" They dropped their guns, and the next thing I knew, I was being taken to hospital in a straitjacket. I spent the night in hospital, and the next day, they gave me some medication to take. Somebody from the hospital helped me find another hotel. All this time, I was wearing only boxer shorts and a hospital gown. A diplomat from the foreign office came out to see me. He asked what all the commotion was. I explained that in Patong, there was a lot more than cricket going on.

I had only a couple of nights left, and I went to visit the James Bond Islands and Phi Phi Island. On the way to one of trips, the conductor, a lady, asked me if I spoke Thai. I answered, "No, why?"

She said, "Because I hear you in Thai." She said she could hear my thoughts. This convinced me that people could indeed hear my thoughts.

I returned home, and as I was at the airport, someone asked whether I would come back to Thailand, to which I answered "No!"

Back in Manchester, I had by now moved to West Didsbury, which was walking distance to work. Because of everything that had gone on, I had the same feeling when I got home that people could hear my thoughts. This led to paranoia. Also, I was told to stop driving since being I had been admitted in Thailand. But this did stop me. At work, I became more and more agitated. I was doing my prescribing course with Dr Blackhall in the small-cell lung cancer clinic. She was a fantastic doctor, working with cutting-edge technology and novel drugs. I was beginning to feel like some sort of prophet again, listening to songs like "If God Was a Man" on repeat.

Then the next event really brought it home that God really did exist, even though I had always believed he did, for God had used me to prove it to others. I was in the pharmacy. A delivery had arrived, and the controlled drugs had to be signed for, so I put my hand in my right trouser pocket, where my pen was. There was no pen there, so I borrowed one and signed for the drugs. Then I handed the pen back. As I was walking back to the dispensary, my right arm went out into the air, and I said, "Here is my pen," and from nowhere, my pen entered my hand. This was definitely a miracle. I remember being angry with God! *Why me?* I thought. *I have always believed.* Then it suddenly dawned on me that all the miracles in the Bible must be true. Everything else that had happened could have been put down to hallucinations, but this was a real physical miracle. People must have seen this, and it must have been caught on CCTV.

A couple of days later, I was in the dispensary, and the locum at the time had left all the difficult checks for me to do. I became annoyed at this and made my opinion known. My manager, Sue, became aware of this, and she called me into the side office of the dispensary. If I kept acting like this, she said, she would take me off the wards. I told her that all the other departments in the hospital worked really hard and were excellent, but the pharmacy was shit! Surprisingly, she agreed. I left the room and thought, *I've had enough.* Without telling anyone, I went off to my GP, Dr Wynn, and explained I needed to be signed off sick. I got an appointment for 5 p.m. Dr Wynn gave me a sick note for stress. I handed this in at 5:30 p.m. to Sue, and she said I had not informed anyone I was leaving work.

The next day, I was wondering what to do, when suddenly, I had idea to go to Germany. I decided I would go to the city where Porsches were made: Stuttgart. Next thing I knew, I was in Stuttgart. I remember getting the train from the airport to the city. As I was getting off the train, I threw away my Bible and Cartier sunglasses. I remember trying to check into the hotel without much luck. Then next thing I knew, I was drinking, and then I must have been shouting in the streets, because I was arrested. The police put me in a cell for one night. I was trying to get their attention to say I needed the toilet, but they never answered. In the end, I had to urinate on the floor.

The next day, they let me out of the cell and charged me around a hundred Euros for the night. I proceeded to throw away my laptop and mobile phone. I remember getting on the tram. I saw an Indian lady there, and I thought, *What is she doing here?* I thought Germany was super racist and had only white people in it. I proceeded to question her about this. The next thing I knew, everyone was disembarking, and the police were getting on to arrest me. They must have realized I was ill because they took me straight to a psychiatric hospital. In the hospital, they asked what medication I was taking. At the time, it was quetiapine. They did blood assays to determine whether I had any in my system. This came back with a zero reading, so they decided to titrate my quetiapine again.

The weekend came, and I asked to have some leave to visit the Porsche Museum. I was granted this. Then, on the Saturday, I was informed that my leave had been cancelled, as the UK police had been in touch and reported me as a missing person. Later, I did get to go to the Porsche Museum. The social worker helped me get a flight back home with the aid of my parents. When I got back to my flat, the door had been kicked in and boarded up by the police, who had been looking for me.

It was around March 2011, and I remember feeling very agitated. One night, I went out into Manchester. After having a few drinks, I left my car in Manchester. I got home and decided to have a shower. I slipped in the shower, and from then on, I did not feel safe on my own in the flat, so I decided to stay at my friend Emer's house, who was just a few streets away. When I got to Emer's house, she was not in. For some reason, I became irate. I had my keys in my hand, and I was walking past a car, I decided to scratch it with my key. Then I thought, *What have I done?* Then I scratched another car, and another, and another. By the time I got home, it must have been ten cars.

Once home, I got my hockey stick out and came back outside. I went across the road and asked the people drinking outside the door, "What shall I do with this?"

They said, "Hit the bin."

So, I went up to the bin and struck it with the hockey stick. They all quickly went inside. I walked down to the end of my street, swinging the hockey stick, taking off car wing mirrors as I went along. I must have damaged ten cars. A BMW was parked in a driveway, and I smashed the back window. An older man came out of the property and started shouting at me. I ignored him and proceeded down the road.

The police turned up, and the officer took the hockey stick off me and put his arm around me. He took me off to the police station, and I was put into a cell. I spent the whole day in there. Then, around 2 p.m., they took me in a police car to identify the damage I had done. Then the next morning, I was taken to Manchester Magistrates court. They decided I could not go back home to Didsbury. I gave them the address of my aunty and uncle in Mobberley. My aunty agreed I could stay, and I was bailed there. I had a curfew of 8 p.m. until 8 a.m.

One day, I thought I would go from my aunty's house to London for the day. I got into my Porsche and started to head towards London. On the way down, I was driving erratically; however, I made it down to Park Lane and decided to check into the Grosvenor Hotel. After I checked into my room and had my car parked in the garage, I decided to walk around and do some shopping. I remember this was payday, so I went into Barclays bank and withdrew £2,000 in cash. I started using taxis to get around. I ended up in jeweller's and put a deposit down on a beautiful gold cross, quite large, with leaves on it.

I ended up at the Savoy Hotel, where I bought myself a ticket for the theatre to watch *Legally Blonde*. Then I walked into the Savoy tailor next to the hotel and bought myself a new suit and shoes to wear to the theatre. At this point, my head was all over the place. I was thinking along the lines that I was a prophet once more. At the forefront of my mind was that Jesus was the one who everyone should follow. I was still thinking people could hear my thoughts. It got so bad that I thought the people who were on TV and radio could hear me. I thought these were special powers. Having people listen to your thoughts made you paranoid and trained your thoughts not to offend anyone by what you were thinking.

I got ready and arrived at the theatre. I decided to have a whisky before the show. They had Jonnie Walker Black Label, which is my father's favourite. The show started, and I was laughing loudly at the jokes, so loudly that some people were looking at me, thinking my behavior bizarre. At the interval, I decided to have more drinks. At first, I thought, *I'll have double.* Then I thought, *I'll have a double for my dad.* Then I thought, *I'll have quadruple for the queen.* I had begun to have a fascination with the royal family, as the queen was the head of the Church of England.

Soon the show was over, and I decided to go back to my hotel. Once there, I remembered that my cousin and his wife were coming back to Manchester from Spain. I had decided I wanted to see them at earliest possible point. I proceeded to reception and asked for my car back. They thought this an odd request, but in the end, they allowed me to drive away in the car. As you can imagine, this was not the best idea I'd had ever had. Not only was my mind mental health impaired due to bipolar disorder, but I'd also had all those drinks.

I remember driving the car very fast up the A5 and proceeding onto M1 northbound. I was driving excessively fast, taking the Porsche to its maximum performance. I had got to Northampton from central London within half an hour. Suddenly, I thought, *When is the junction for M6 going to appear?* I took my foot off the accelerator. Then that was it! The engine of the Porsche blew out of the back of the car. Even at this speed, I knew it was not my time to go yet, so I held the steering wheel as tightly as I could and shut my eyes. The result was the car hit the central reservation. All the airbags went off, and the hood was ripped off. The car came to a standstill. My first reaction was to get out and head to the hard shoulder. As I was walking across the motorway, a policeman came up to me, cuffed me, and threw me into the back of a police car.

Luckily, my only injuries were a friction burn to my right wrist where the airbag had caught it and a cut to the back of my head. At the police station, they got someone to see me who usually sees to family of the bereaved. They said it was a miracle I had got out alive.

At the police station, I was given a solicitor. When I was questioned, I told them I was only going 90 miles per hour. The officer had told me earlier they had chased me but could not catch up. People were ringing in saying there was a Porsche travelling in excess of 150 mph. The solicitor told me the engine of the car was half a mile behind where the body had come to a standstill. Anyhow, I was bailed to come back on the 4 July.

It was daytime, and I remember only having the change in my pocket. I rang my uncle and told him I was stranded in Northampton. He told me he could not come that day. The next day, however, on the Sunday, my father came to pick me up. It was one of the most bizarre nights I had spent on the streets. Somehow, an older lady had tagged on to me. She could probably see I was distressed and tried to help. She took me back to what seemed like a council apartment. She could see that my shirt was full of blood and gave me a T-shirt to change into. In the morning, we went to church, but I couldn't sit through the whole service, as I was hearing all sorts of voices, which left me agitated.

I got in touch with my father, and he said, "Just stay at the police station."

I went back there and waited for him. It had been over twenty-four hours since I had eaten. We stopped at the service station and got food. I remember feeling elated, thinking everyone knew I was a prophet. Soon enough, I was back at my uncle's house. As I looked out my bedroom window, it seemed as if there were a moat around the property. The next morning, I was being interviewed by the mental-health team. I went back to Stepping Hill Hospital in Stockport.

Once I got onto the ward, I remember a Bible being on the table, it was getting bigger in front of my eyes. I remember thinking this was to add my life events to end of it. For now, however, I was stuck in hospital, waiting for the inevitable to happen, which was my worst nightmare: being put back onto depot injection medication. At first, I resisted this, but my family persuaded me this was the only medication that would work for me. As I was not willing to have the depot, a team of nurses would come into my bedroom and forcibly administer the dose, at which point, I gave in and just let them inject me. This time, it was a drug called Modecate. At first, I had a few side effects, like a clicking jaw. However, they were not interested in my complaints, and I was made to continue.

To add insult to injury, they decided I would need a mood stabilizer, in the form of sodium valproate tablets. This had the unfortunate side effect of thinning my hair. After three months, I received my discharge by way of hospital community treatment order. This meant if did not attend my appointment for the depot medication, I would be recalled to hospital. After all this upheaval, I would be up against the General Pharmaceutical Society again. Their lawyers would argue my fitness to practice was impaired. The judge and panel agreed, and this would mean I was suspended from practising for twelve months.

At this point, I was still employed by Christie Hospital, but my contract would come to an end, and still, I had not been able to get back on the register as a practising pharmacist. These were some of the most depressing times of my life. So, unable to work as a pharmacist, I decided to get some qualifications as an accountant and work for my father.

CHAPTER 13

ACCOUNTANCY AND THEOLOGY

I would enrol in a private college that trained accountants, taking the ACCA course. These were really bad times. I kept wondering, *Why me?* The highs were brilliant, but the low moods brought to the greatest depths of my life. The college I was enrolled in was in Manchester city centre. I remember getting the train in the morning and evening. Every time I stood on the platform at the train station, I had suicidal thoughts, wondering if I should just throw myself into the path of the train. I hated life at this point. My weight went through the roof, and I was hardly recognizable. It seemed everything was against me. Each day was a struggle, and the strong antipsychotic medication made it difficult to study.

The one thing that kept me going was the knowledge that God was real and this has been proven beyond doubt. Before the pen incident, all the miracles could have been put down to hallucinations, but this miracle defied the very laws of physics. After one year of accountancy school, I managed to pass the first three exams.

The year was up, and I would be able to go before the pharmacy board again. This time, the judging panel would still find my fitness to practice impaired, but they would now allow me to practise, with conditions. It would be difficult to find employment with these conditions. However, I was persistent. It was 2011 when I had my car crash, and it would be 2014 before I would gain employment as a pharmacist again. Looking back, I was fortunate to gain employment at Manchester Royal Infirmary. I had pestered the clinical deputy chief pharmacist to give me an opportunity. Then they called me in for interview, and I was appointed as a bank pharmacist.

The clinical side of this job would be fine, I was happy clinically checking prescriptions and advising doctors on the ward, but the bulk of the work on the wards was medicines reconciliation, which was ascertaining what medicines patients were on. Overall, it was a tedious task that which I thought was below me and should have been carried out by clerical staff.

Even in this job, I was not happy, as I was getting paid as a junior pharmacist and had to do a tedious job. My career as a pharmacist had been shattered by my illness. Then, one day, while on the ward, I had to do an audit of the controlled-drugs cupboard. A senior nurse and I conducted the audit and found that there was a full bottle of morphine missing. We emptied the cupboard and put everything back, and still, there was the missing bottle. Even one of the doctors had a look and agreed it was missing. We took this information to the nurse in charge of the ward. She said we would have to put in a critical incident form. She asked us to check one more time, so the nurse I conducted the audit again, opening the cabinet. The missing bottle was sitting just next to the open one. This freaked the nurse out. However, by now, I was used to this—with the ring, the pen, and now this.

I decided this was a sign from God that I must look to other avenues for my career. I was utterly disheartened by pharmacy. My heart was in service to God. After all, it seemed that he kept showing me signs to follow him. So, I decided to investigate studying theology, which is the study of religion, specifically the Bible. I looked for courses on the internet. Most universities taught theology; however, these were mostly for students who were going to university after finishing their A levels. Then I found a course at Trinity College Bristol, a college mainly for Ordinands of the Church of England who would go on to be vicars. I looked at this course, and there seemed to be a lot of contact time, which appealed to me.

In June 2015, I decided I would apply to Trinity college Bristol. After a formal interview, I was accepted in their undergraduate degree course. The course would entail tuition fees and living fees, which would amount to around £16,000 each year. This led me to the decision to sell my flat in Leeds and use the money released to go to university. However, the flat in Leeds did not sell straight away, so I took a holiday to Pakistan for the whole month of August. When I got back, I had two weeks to work at Manchester Royal Hospital, and then it would be time to go to university. The problem was I did not have the funds to pay the fees or for living accommodation. As the date loomed nearer, I convinced my brother to let me borrow £5,000 just so I could go to Bristol and pay the first instalment for fees. When I went to Bristol, I was still on the Modecate depot injection. This had made me put on weight, and but apart from this side effect, I seemed to be doing OK. My mental health was good at this point. I was suffering from only one other side effect: my thoughts had slowed down, and my ability to concentrate was impaired.

My parents drove me down to Bristol. When they saw the Christian ethos of the college, they were not impressed. However, when I arrived at the college, fellow students were there to greet me. The residence called Carter Hall, and about eighteen of us singletons would be residing there. I would make good friends with two lovely guys who were slightly older than me. One was Dan, who had served as a missionary in Afghanistan, and the other was Ed, who had trained as a barrister and been working lately lately as a solicitor.

The first night, we all decided to walk to the nearest pub for a drink. This is when I started to talk to Dan for the first time. He told me briefly about his time in Afghanistan. He told me a story which stick in my mind that I'll share with you. Basically, while in Afghanistan, Dan had a driver who had converted from Islam to Christianity. He told a story of when he was driving his car along a rocky road, when suddenly, his car broke down. This was a deserted area, and footfall traffic was low. He was on his own in the car. The car had broken down under some rocks. The driver fell asleep in the car. Late at night, he heard a knock on the window. It was a man dressed all in white. He asked the man to move the car slightly down the road. He explained to the man that the car had broken down. The man said to him, "Just try."

He turned the ignition, and the car started. He moved the car twenty metres down the road. He got out, looked around, and the man had vanished. He fell asleep again. Then he heard a thunderous noise. He woke up to find that where the car had originally broken down, there had been a landslide of rocks covering the road. Later, the man asked an Islamic scholar who this man in white, who had saved his life, might have been. He replied, "Don't repeat this, but it must have been 'Isa,'" which is the Arabic for Jesus. As soon as Dan mentioned Jesus, I felt pins and needles all over my body, with a feeling of warmth. This was the first time I felt the Holy Spirit.

College life was all very nice. The people were lovely Christians and quite conservative overall. Monday to Friday, we went to a service in the chapel at college. Lectures were interesting. Everything seemed to be going well, as it was the first time I had felt positive about life in a long time. I was beginning to enjoy life again. The only problem was I was feeling lethargic and not performing very well in my essays. In October 2015, I went to see my GP and asked with his consent if I could come off the Modecate, because of the side effects I was suffering, and try a newer oral medication. He agreed, and I was put on oral aripiprazole.

Suddenly, I felt I was in control of my life again. I lost weight and felt better. I used to cash in the prescription every month, but I thought I could control my life better without the medication, and so I did not take the tablets. Around Christmastime, I went back home to Stockport. While there, I got some of my test results, which weren't very good. I began to doubt whether my decision to sell the flat and pursue a career in theology was a good idea. Still, the flat had not sold, but over Christmas, I finally got an offer on it, which I accepted.

When I got back to Bristol, I decided now that I had the funds, I would join the college trip to the Holy Land, Israel. Even though I had been there before, I was really excited about this trip. Everything was going well. Life was good, and I had almost forgotten that I had bipolar disorder. I had lost weight by going to the gym and swimming, sometimes twice a day. I was doing the odd locum shift as a pharmacist as well as my studies. Then the time came to visit Israel. There would be twelve of us going on the trip. I drove in my car with two others to the airport. We managed to book our Easyjet flight to Tel Aviv. The flight there was unremarkable, and we landed four and a half hours later. Everyone else on the trip made it through immigration, but I was asked to stay behind for more information.

The rest of the group headed to the hotel, and Peter, who organized the trip, stayed behind to wait for me. After an interrogation about my reasons for visiting Israel, which took about one and a half hours, they were finally satisfied and let me out. This was my first planned trip to Israel this year. I had also planned another for six months to work for a charitable trust in a hospital in Nazareth, for the Nazareth Trust. We visited Jericho and the Dead Sea. At this time, I began to feel elated, but overall I felt fine. Most of the time while on the trip, we were in double-occupancy rooms, and so I would get some sleep. Then we got to the Sea of Galilee, and I had my own room. This meant I had more freedom. When everyone would be asleep, I would go out and start praying in the abandoned synagogue. This was when I started hearing voices. They were a mixture, but mainly now it was Liz (the girl I met in Sheffield), God, and Jesus. My head felt like a telephone exchange. I was having a conversation in my head with four people at some points. Thoughts were racing. This led me to believe I was some sort of prophet again.

Then from Galilee, we went to Jerusalem. As I was on the coach and we were entering the city, I began to get excited. Our coach dropped us off just outside the city wall, and we dragged our bags to the hotel within the walls. The first thing I wanted to do was go to the Western Wall, so left the rest of the group and started praying at the Western Wall. Then, as I was walking back to the accommodation, some called out to me, "King."

I ignored him; however, I had the feeling I was closer to God than anyone and was, in fact, the new King of the Jews. By this time, I thought people could hear my thoughts again. I could tell I was falling ill again but could not resist the euphoria of this high.

Then I thought I needed some time to myself, so I went to the King David Hotel and checked in there for three days. The hotel was beautiful. I remember going to bar one night and ordering a whisky. The girl behind the bar advised me that it cost eighty pounds for a single. I felt more energetic than usual and was sleeping only two to three hours per night. One night, at around eleven o'clock, I decided to walk down to the Western Wall to pray. I had my passport on me, and when I got stopped by the guards at the entrance to the wall, I produced this as proof of identification. I remember having to bribe them to get past at that time of night, as usually, only Jews would be praying at this time.

Things became very bizarre. The group leader, from the organized college tour, was wondering whether I would be joining them for any of the scheduled tours. We agreed I would join them for one service, which was to be held at the crypt of accommodation they were staying in. I spent time wandering around Jerusalem, focusing my time on the Western Wall. I felt like Jerusalem was a haven for spirituality. I felt closer to God there than anywhere else on earth. After all, it was the epicentre for the Abrahamic religions.

One night, as I was walking back from the Western Wall I walked in a straight line for around five minutes. I realized I was somewhere unfamiliar. The hotel was in a straight line from the Jaffa Gate. The sun started to rise, and I asked a local man who was out walking which direction the King David Hotel was in. He pointed me in the right direction but explained it was still quite far away. The next night was the last scheduled night in Israel, and the following morning, we were all. Peter, the group leader, got in touch with me and asked whether I would be joining them on the coach back to the airport. I told him I was planning to stay in Jerusalem a little while longer.

Later that evening, I went to pray at the Western Wall again, and once again, on the way back late at night, I found myself lost. I had walked into a suburb of Jerusalem after walking five minutes in a straight line. It was though I were being teleported to a different area without knowing it. I found myself at a small row of shops. I walked into the fruit and veg shop for something to eat. I picked up an apple and asked the owner how much it was. He said it was free. Then I walked into a barbershop. I was trying to explain that I was very thirsty and asked for water. They replied, "You mean pani?" which meant water in Urdu. Then, suddenly, I thought I had a flight back to England and should board it. I got a taxi back to the hotel, which took about fifteen minutes, when it only took five minutes to walk there.

I quickly packed all my belongings from the room and checked out. I decided to get a taxi to airport. Once I was at the airport, there was the whole thing at security, being questioned about every little detail of my trip and why

I had left the group. They asked how I could afford to stay in the King David hotel. I managed to get through security. I had about 2,000 Israeli shekels in my wallet, and then a voice in my head said, "Count the money." I counted it, and it was 2,000. Then the voice said, "Leave it on the table," so I left it on the table and walked away.

A couple of minutes later, I thought I might need that money, so I walked back to the table, and the money was gone. Then, as I walked away from the table, I felt a little tap on my jeans pocket where my wallet was located. I took my wallet out of the pocket, opened it, and the 2,000 Israeli shekels were there. By now, I was used to miracles and just took it on the chin and carried on.

On the flight back from Tel Aviv, my thoughts were racing. I was glad when we got back to Stanstead, London. My thoughts at this point were all over the place, and I was convinced when the plane landed, I would be taken to hospital. I managed to get through the airport without any bother, but I had forgotten which car park my car had been in. I got the airport bus to the car park farthest away, and luckily, after walking around for about half an hour, I managed to find my car.

I decided to go back to Bristol. I got into my car in a slightly agitated frame of mind and set off. By this time, it was late at night, and it was more difficult to navigate the way back home to university. I remember feeling elated, closer to God, and felt as though Judaism was the right religion while also accepting Jesus. I had made a post on Facebook which defined my religious beliefs as Messianic Jew. While I was in Israel, I had also bought a gold pendant, which was the sign of the Messianic Jewish Church.

This is a picture of me sporting the messianic Jewish seal.

The next thing I knew, it was edging towards 8 a.m. I know this because eventually, my car ran out of petrol on the M27 in Southampton. I abandoned the car on the hard shoulder of the motorway and walked about five minutes down the road. I was in a town, and the shops were not open. It happened again. I would realize afterwards that I was more than two miles away from my where my car broke down, while it took only five minutes to walk. Anyhow, the next thing I knew, a police officer had accosted me. He was asking what I was doing there, and had I been shouting out aloud in public? Then he asked if I suffered from any mental health issues. I told him my car was just down the road. He took me in his car, and two minutes down the road was a petrol station. He stopped there. I asked if I could purchase some food and drink. He declined and said he was holding me under the Mental Health Act. At this point, I had not eaten for forty-eight hours while in Jerusalem.

From there, they took me to some secure institution in Southampton. I was locked in the room, which had two windows, one looking into the nurses' station and the other looking outside at a wall. The wall had Hebrew writing on it. At one point, I was looking in a corner mirror in the room, and through the image in the mirror, I could see the back of a man dressed in a red-hooded robe standing in the room. However, I could not see him in front of me. They still had not managed to give me any medication or any food or drink. Then I saw through the window at the nurses' station two Jewish men, observing me. After a while, they began to smoke. Awhile later, I lay down on the slab in the middle of the room and fell asleep.

The next morning, they came into the room and gave me some medication and informed me I was being transferred. They gave me two packs of sandwiches as we left in a private ambulance. As I looked at the wall where the Hebrew writing had been, it looked as if it had been pulled off. I was admitted to a mental health ward at the private hospital in Weston-super-Mare. As soon as I got there, I accepted the medication they gave me, and they started me back on the aripiprazole. Luckily, it was not too far from Bristol, and I had visits from my personal tutor and from my fellow student friends. After around ten days, I was discharged back to the community.

At around this time I started to think again about the girl Liz from the Sheffield Hotel. So, I would stay up late at night searching on the internet for her. All I knew was she studied English Literature and was twenty years old when I met her, and she was Catholic. At the same time, I was trying to get some locum with Lloyds Pharmacy, which did not go well, as I had some conditions on my registration. Around this time, two things happened—I found a potential match for Liz, who was now living in Essex, near Cambridge. The other thing was that I was not satisfied with not being able to locum for Lloyds, so I thought I would take it up with their Celsio head office in Munich. On a whim, I organized flights to go out from Heathrow to Munich and then thought I would drive down to Stuttgart and fly back from there.

CHAPTER 14

MANIA AND CHAOS

Around June, I started to spend more time in the Cambridge area, looking for Liz. I came across the town of Saffron Walden, which was very nice and close to where this Liz lived. I would stay in the lovely little village of Thaxted. For a while, I was back and forth between Bristol and Cambridgeshire. I also became fond of a local stately manor house in Cambridgeshire, called Audley End. I would spend time just relaxing in the gardens. Then, one day, I did the house tour, looking at the books in the library, one one of the staff asked if I would like to sit down and read. One day, I had an altercation with some people in Thaxted. The police were called, and I had to move out. So, I went to the Hilton Hotel in Cambridge city centre.

I was off my medication again. My thoughts were flying, and I was unable to control them. I rang up the Celsio head office and talked to a chap called Andreas. I told him I was coming over to Germany, and he said he was supposed to be in England then, but if I was coming, he would stay in Germany. I remember we had great difficulty exchanging e-mails. I had not told anyone what I was planning and jetted off to Munich.

When I landed in Munich, I was surprised to see that in the arrivals, there was a duty-free section. I ended up buying a red ladies Porsche bag and some Cartier sunglasses, among other items.

Then from the airport, I hired a Mercedes. I drove into Munich, found my way to the Alliance Arena, had a quick walk around, and went to find a hotel. I checked into the hotel, had a quick bite to eat, and then went for a drive on the Autobahn. I was driving very erratically and very fast. Suddenly, I felt as if I needed to get back to England, so I headed back to Munich Airport, parked the car in front of the departure gate, and went to the Lufthansa travel desk to enquire about a new ticket. The only one they had was a business-class ticket for one thousand pounds. At the time, I just wanted to get home, so I bought the ticket.

When I got back to England, I landed at Heathrow. From there, I went to hire a car from Avis. They told me they had Porsche, which required a £3,000 deposit. I thought was a bit expensive. In the end, I opted for a Mercedes E class. I paid the initial rental for two days and signed the contract for hire. I remember the person saying, "Make sure you hand it back in time." I told them I would hand it back to the Sheffield depot, as I was planning to go to Chatsworth. I'd had a fascination with Chatsworth House ever since I met Liz at the Sheffield Hotel. We had arranged to meet near there, at Fischer's restaurant at Baslow Hall, Derbyshire, which is in the vicinity of Chatsworth. So, for some reason, I added two and two together and got ten. I thought this Liz I had met had something to do with the Cavendish family of Chatsworth.

I proceeded to drive out of London, but along the way, I kept getting lost. Also, the SAT NAV in the car was not working properly, and this meant I was getting confused and lost. I kept ending up at the entrance of a hospital. No matter which route I took, I would end up back there. In the end, I decided to take the route I knew out of London. So, I drove back into the centre to Hyde Park Corner and proceeded up the A5 and then M1. Once on the motorway, I stopped at the first services and stopped over in the hotel. All I remember is that it was late and I was tired, with all sorts of voices and paranoid thoughts going through my mind.

At some point, I thought I could communicate with Liz through my psychic powers. I started talking to myself with her. I would be talking out loud, in my own voice, followed by the voice of a girl. I got to the village of Pilsley, within the grounds of the Chatsworth Estate, and checked into the Devonshire Arms. I was given the Dunsa Room. As I went up to my room, I started behaving oddly (hence, talking in two different voices—my own and that of a girl, whom I thought was Liz).

I was acutely ill. I would spend my days in the village of Bakewell driving back and forth from the hotel. While I was in Bakewell, I went into the local jeweller's, C. W. Sellors, and proceeded to buy diamond earrings and a Mikimoto pearl necklace. I would also then spend time at Chatsworth and proceeded to gift the duke a bottle of Oban 14 whisky. Then I mentioned to the staff that I had a present for the duchess. I was going to give her the diamond earrings I had bought, but they said they could not accept the gift, even if it was a diamond necklace.

Then, one night, I got back to the hotel late, and they had shut the entrance. I had no option but to sleep in the car. I proceeded to put on the music in the car, which later, I was told that been quite loud, disturbing the other residents. During this night, I thought I would take the car back to Sheffield. So, late at night (or early in the morning), I would start driving back to Sheffield. While I was driving, I realized the lights on the car had stopped working unless I put on the full beams. So, there I was, driving down the country lanes without lights, just flashing my full beams from time to time. While I was on the road, hordes of birds flew in front of my car, ticking off again just in time.

I got to Sheffield and parked the car in the multistorey car park next to the main train station. I left the car there then proceeded to the St Pauls Hotel, Sheffield, where I would try to get a room for the night. But they were fully booked and referred me to the Hilton. So, I stayed there for a few hours that night. Early the next morning, I got into a taxi and made my way back to Pilsley. I got to the hotel and was informed that I had to check out, as there were no room for additional nights. So, I asked if someone could help me pack. They helped me pack and called a taxi. The taxi arrived, and I got my belongings and left for Sheffield to get the train back to Stockport. However, on the way to Sheffield I saw a Land Rover garage and asked the driver to stop, and I jumped out of the taxi and went into the showroom and apparently tried to buy a Discovery. Anyhow, the taxi driver left me there and, then I got another taxi back to Devonshire Arms. When I got back there, there was a brief confrontation, as I believed the taxi had run off with my belongings. Then they called the taxi back, and Chatsworth security turned up. They handed me back the bottle of whisky I had given to the duke. I must have been questioning them about the queen's visit, and they proceeded to tell me she only visited once every five years. The next thing I knew, the taxi turned up. I paid him about forty pounds to get my belongings back, and then swiftly, the police arrived.

I was taken to Chesterfield police station, where they treated me like some sort of terrorist. In the end, they granted me bail and told me would need to attend later. They kept hold of my laptop to see there was no terrorist activity on there. By this time, it was around 24 June. I remember this because it was my brother Wahib's birthday. I gathered all my belonging from the police and got a taxi to Stockport, to my parents' house. When I got home, I went into a local pub, called The Griffin. Here, I was elated and proceeded to show people the pearls and diamonds I had bought. And because I was hearing voices, especially that of Liz, I proceeded to tell people I was going to marry her. This is how confused a person with mental illness can get.

I noticed that two men in the pub had started paying me a lot of attention. In hindsight, this was because I was parading around with thousands of pounds of jewellery. Then they were buying me shots and telling me they could go anywhere in the world, whenever they wanted. So, I said, "Let's go. I want to go to New York." They backtracked and tried to get hold of my briefcase containing the jewellery. I managed to get my briefcase back and then made a sharp exit to the airport. I got to the airport and realized I did not have a ticket for New York. On my phone, I called Hilton Hotels in New York and booked accommodation. I asked if I needed a visa, and they informed me it could be issued at the airport. Unusually for me at this time, I would be dressed in a suit. Usually, I would only wear these when I was at work.

I booked into the airport hotel, and in the hotel bar, I got talking to a gentleman. I advised him I was trying to book a flight to New York but finding it difficult to book on my phone. He had a look on his laptop and found a flight out in the morning, via Brussels. I managed to book the flight on my phone and then, the next morning, boarded the flight to Brussels. I had my briefcase with me and my connecting boarding pass. Then, as I approached the gate for the flight to New York, I was asked if I had an ESTA, to which I answered "no." They told me there was still time and to use one of the terminal computers. So, I was running through the airport, suited and booted. Then I managed to get onto one of the computer terminals, and what should have taken me less than five minutes to fill out ended up taking twenty minutes, by which time, the gate was closed.

Then I thought I would go to the American embassy in Brussels to see if they could help with the ESTA. Anyway, it was a wasted journey into the city centre. You had to be an American national to gain access.

In the end, I decided to go back to the airport and booked into the attached hotel. I got some rest there, and then I had another brainwave, so I decided to fly to Stuttgart, Germany. I managed to book a flight to Stuttgart, which was leaving that day. So, I got to the airport terminal, rushing to catch my flight. After boarding the flight, I began to relax. I fell asleep on the flight, which did not take long to get to its destination. When we landed in Stuttgart, there was a lightning storm. We had to stay on the airplane as lightning lit up the evening sky. While I was on the airplane, I booked my hotel, the Steinbergerer Graf Zeppelin Hotel, opposite the central train station. I got a taxi from the airport down to the hotel.

I checked in to the hotel and slept through the night. In the morning, I went down to the restaurant for breakfast. All was going well so far; I didn't think they suspected I was suffering from any mania. I still thought people could hear my thoughts, but I tried my best to keep it real. I could tell the staff suspected something was wrong. At lunchtime, I proceeded to hotel bar and ordered a fillet steak for my lunch and asked to eat it at the bar. This was fine, and they accommodated that request. After this, I had $500, which I had taken out for New York, so I decided I would give this money as a tip to a couple of staff. This must have seemed odd to them. Then I went across the road to the where the train station was and checked in to the intercity Stuttgart Hotel. I checked in here just because I was not getting a good vibe from my hotel. Then I proceeded to put in their safety deposit box the pearls and earrings I had.

After this, I went back across the road to the Steinbergerer Hotel, and as I went to the bar, I saw a gentleman going up the stairs who looked like Mohammed Al Fayyad. At this time, I was fascinated with Princess Diana and was convinced it was the French authorities who had let her die, by failing to provide enough security. Anyhow, I didn't give it second thought and asked for an Oban 14 whisky. However, it did not matter how clearly I asked for the whisky; they kept asking "Which one?" as if they couldn't understand me. In the end, I pointed up to the whisky, but still, the attendant would not get me the Oban 14. Anyway, the next thing I knew, I was being asked to leave the hotel, so I checked out and went to the hotel across the road.

While at the intercity hotel, I took back my jewellery from the safety deposit box. Later that night, as I left the hotel with my briefcase, which had the jewellery in, I saw a procession of police, so I decided to follow them, and this led me to a student union bar. Here at the bar, I asked them to look after my briefcase. A young lady took the briefcase for me and said she would look after it. Once again, it seemed people could hear my thoughts. While I was at the bar, I remember thinking that since we were leaving Europe, I did not need my English money anymore and proceeded to set some notes on fire. Some students questioned what I was doing, and they proceeded to put the flames out and take the money.

At some point during these days in Stuttgart, I went shopping. I went into a Swarovski shop, and within ten minutes, I was pointed out to the attendant, Julia which items I wanted. All in all, I ended up spending five thousand Euros in ten minutes. As I could not carry all these items, I asked them to keep them there for myself while I got some baggage to put them in. I proceed to buy two suitcases. Also in frenzy of spending, I bought three watches, two of which were identical, for a sum of six thousand Euros.

After I got back into the intercity hotel, I can remember looking outside my window and across the road at what should have been the Steinbergerer Hotel, but there were only trees in what looked like a park. I looked to the left, and the hotel was there. It seemed the hotel had moved places. Then I remember looking in the morning again, and it was across the road again. Obviously, my mind had started playing games with my vision, or God was doing things only he could. I remember on this night, I was thinking about the queen of England, and as I thought I was the king of the Jews, I thought I could communicate with her. As I was communicating telepathically to the queen and Jesus, I felt a burning sensation on the bottom of my feet, as though the skin beneath was bubbling. There must have been some link between the psychological and the physiological. At this time, I thought the UK was going to send people to come and take me back to England. I thought I needed to send an SOS message and proceeded to throw a glass bottle of water out my bedroom window onto the road, but nobody came to get me.

I managed to get a few hours' sleep that night, then proceeded out into the city. I found myself walking around aimlessly. I came across an early morning market. Then I became suspicious that people were following me. These paranoid delusions were taking their toll on my already broken, confused mind. I became disorientated and could not find my way back to the hotel, so I entered a building site and started walking around it. Then I saw a fire alarm. I proceeded to break the glass and set off the alarm. Everyone vacated the building (it was mainly construction workers). Then, with all sorts of voices going through my head, I picked up a stone and threw it at one of the construction workers. Then all these young men who seemed to be following me ran towards me. At first, I ran away, but they caught up with me and pinned me against the floor. They put so much pressure on my legs, I thought they would break them. The pain was excruciating.

The police came and took me into custody. Even in the cell, I could feel the pain in my legs. Slowly, after about ten minutes, the pain subsided, as if they were miraculously healed. The police took me to a hospital. The first one did not accept me. Then I was taken to a private hospital—in fact, the same one as in 2011.

At the hospital, I was eager to be released and get back to England. Unfortunately, while I was there, things didn't go well. I accepted that I needed medication and took the aripiprazole. However, I felt I was not being treated well and needed help from the British embassy. When I contacted the embassy, the hospital staff were not very happy. In the end, there was a confrontation, and they ended up putting me in a straightjacket, then lay there, strapped onto the bed. Two nurses were with me, one male, one female. As the female one came near, I moved my arm towards her. The male nurse took this as a sign of aggression and proceeded to strangle me. As he was doing this, I did not flinch, so he punched me in the eye socket. Thankfully, I was not hurt. I reported this to the embassy.

Then the people from the embassy came, and I had what I assumed was a tribunal in German. They deemed I did not need to be on a section, and I agreed to stay informally. I was given leave and appointed a social worker. The social worker helped me get back my belongings from the hotel. Then we tried to find the bar where my briefcase was, but I was unsuccessful. It had my passport in there, so there was a bit of a problem. Then I was given leave on my own recognizance, so I went back to the intercity hotel and retraced my steps to the bar. As soon as I walked in, the girl behind the bar recognized me. She said, "I've still got your bag," and gave it back to me. Everything was still in there. I gave her a tip with my only remaining Israeli shekels.

Now that I had my passport back, I managed to book a flight back to London. I had my belongings and proceeded back to England. Even when I got back home to the UK, I did not feel one hundred per cent well. I remember getting in my car and driving back to Manchester. On the way back, I was stopped by police. They said I had been reported missing and that is why there was an alert on my car. I arrived back in Stockport. I stayed here for a while before I found my way back to Cambridge. Here, I would spend the days in the sunshine, with a little shopping, and I even did the touristy river cruise. Then things started to get bizarre again. I remember being on a night out on my own and joining a group of lads, buying champagne and sharing it as if administering Communion. One day, I bought an expensive blazer from Ede and Ravenscroft. Then I took out five hundred pounds from the bank and started giving away money to street performers, one hundred pounds at a time.

I decided I would travel to Israel again, so I went to the travel agent, and they booked the holiday for just three days. My flights were with British Airways, from Heathrow, so I made my way to London. I was booked in a Holiday Inn at the airport. When I arrived, I booked in and went up to the room to leave my luggage. When I came back to the lounge area, there was a football match, and I decided to watch. I noticed there was a Punjabi wedding going on in the function room. I entered the room and asked the DJ to put on a song. As I walked out of the function room, I was shouting, "*Apna Punjab*," which means "our Punjab". Obviously, this annoyed the wedding party. Then they made a complaint against me, and I was asked to leave the hotel.

I got back into my car and found a Premier Inn hotel nearby. When I checked for my bank card, it was missing. Luckily, I had a lot of change and managed to pay for the room with cash. Early the next morning, I got the airport bus to Terminal 5, where the flight was due to depart. Onboard the flight, I had a feeling my bank card would come back to me. Midflight, I checked my wallet, and my bank card was miraculously there again.

I had booked the King David Hotel again for two nights. I checked in and knew most of the staff. They were pleased to see me. The weather was amazing, and I spent most of the day by the pool, only occasionally venturing out of the hotel to visit the shops or the Western Wall. This mini-break went along without any hiccups, until I was in a jewellery shop and my card got declined. There were thousands in the account, but the card would not work. I could not believe it.

It came time to leave Israel. As I checked out of the hotel, I was informed the room had not yet been paid for and that I owed $1,800. The payment did not go through. The hotel was trying all sorts of things to put the payment through and would not let me go without paying the bill. I was in a bit of a pickle. I rang home to my parents, and the hotel spoke to my parents. However, by this time, my parents were sick of bailing me out. They refused to pay the bill. I had a flight to catch. It was all quite embarrassing. In the end, they took me to the office, but there was just no way to pay the bill. In the end, they let me go. I got in a taxi and had only enough shekels to pay for the ride to the airport.

I arrived at the airport, late for my flight, which had departed. The only thing I could do was to buy a new ticket. I was stuck in Israel at the airport without any money and no way of getting back home. In the end, I pleaded with my parents to help me buy a ticket back to Manchester. They agreed, as they knew there was no other way to get home.

The first week seemed to go well, but after the weekend, I went to the pub, and in there, I started to feel paranoid and fell out with people. I called my mum to give me a lift. I waited a while, but she was a no-show, so I decided to walk home, about a fifteen-minute walk. As I was walking home, the heavens opened, to the point where I was absolutely soaked. As I walked up our drive, my mum pulled up also. I was in such a rage as my brother got out of the car that I kicked him and fell to the ground. I began shouting at him and my mother. Eventually, the police were called. I ended up being taken to Stepping Hill Hospital's mental health unit.

It was September 2016. I was looking at a long stretch in the hospital again. The doctor allocated to me was an Irish lady. She was very stern, adamant that I go onto depot medication again. There was only one way out of this situation: the same old game of *yes sir, no sir*. Just do everything they ask. So, I quickly accepted the depot medication on the condition it would be newer Abilify, aripiprazole, or depot medication. The doctor agreed but was unhappy and wanted me to go on a mood stabilizer. I was put on sodium valproate again. The last time I was put on this, it had thinned my hair. I was very reluctant, but in the end, I had no choice. My hair suffered as a result. My weight went up. I felt lethargic.

The doctor was still not happy, and she did not want me discharged to my parents' address, instead wanting me to go to sheltered housing, with nursing care. I was furious at this suggestion and adamant this was not going to happen. Then I got the break I was looking for. My doctor went off sick. I was assessed for the sheltered housing but deemed not to fit their criteria. My next plan was to escape the community treatment order. By this time, it was December. When the new doctor appeared on the ward, I could not believe it—he was a family friend from Pakistan, who had come over to do some locums! At the hospital, we did not let on that we knew each other. He gave me some time at home to test the waters. I was on a section 3, which is a six-month section. My tribunal hearing was due for early January.

I was given some time out over Christmas, and on Christmas Day, my parents had invited this doctor around for our family Christmas dinner. In the tribunal, I was on form. Directed by my solicitor, Mr O'Donnell, I said very little as evidence was given out. Then I had my say, which I kept short and sweet. The doctor was going off previous recommendations, but he was very ambiguous, which was good for me. Then the panel deliberated, and the outcome was that I was taken off my section with immediate effect, and the judge deemed there was no need for a community treatment order.

Now, this was not the only problem. While I was in Derbyshire, they charged me with racial and religious public order offences. I was advised by my solicitor, "Just plead guilty."

Once again, I had to deal with the General Pharmaceutical Council. My fitness to practise was found to be impaired, and I was suspended from the register. So, I was in the same predicament again: jobless. My bipolar disorder had taken its toll on my career. The first time I went up against the board, the issue was that I had not been taking my sodium valproate, as prescribed. So, they said I was not complying with the treatment plan. They said they would see me after six months.

Six months went by, and I had sorted out with my treating team that I did not need the sodium valproate. This time, when I went up against the board, a neutral solicitor came to see me. He advised me that the first thing the committee need to ascertain was whether my fitness to practise was impaired. He persuaded me to say it was not. Anyhow, it was the best advice I could have been given. The committee judged that my fitness to practise was not impaired.

CHAPTER 15

THE FINAL MANIC EPISODE

I managed to get a job with Lloyds Pharmacy in Cadishead, northwest Manchester, which started in January 2019. So, I had been off for two and half years again. My professional life as a pharmacist had been a disaster. I had done bits of everything but not really stuck at anything. Here I was, a community pharmacist again. I was enjoying being back at work. I had my driver's licence back, and things were looking up. However, all the time I had spent on bipolar missions had taken their toll on me. I was older, with nothing to show for myself. This began to get me down. However, all the miracles and adventures I had been on gave me a belief in God that was unremarkable. I had seen the miracles. It's not all about science. I had been shown firsthand by God that science can be redefined.

By now I could control these voices in my head. They remained absent for long periods. However, in April 2019, one night, after a few too many double espressos, I could not sleep, and the voices came back. They were not as intense as they first were. At first, I just got a bit more emotional. Then, I started to talk to Jesus and God. These would be three-way conversations. In May 2019, I had a review with my psychiatrist and decided to come off the depot on and transition to oral medication. As I had breakthrough symptoms even on the depot, I thought the medication wasn't necessary, and it was divine the thoughts I was having. I stopped the medication altogether.

Around September 2019, I decided to move out of my parents' house. At the same time, I went for an interview for a job in primary care. My thoughts at the moment were fine. I was managing to keep everything together. I was accepted for the job in primary care. This gave me a chance to hand in my notice at Lloyds. I moved into my flat in Didsbury, Manchester, in early October. I finished work at Lloyds at the end of October. Around the time I moved into the flat, I started a new relationship with a nurse, Emma, whom I had met on the internet. Things were looking up. I was looking forward to a starting a job I wanted, in a relationship, and living independently. I had to start all over again when it came to furnishing the flat. The bank gave me a credit card. I was in between jobs. I had savings, but my lifestyle away from work was exorbitant without any money coming in. I started spending on my credit card, and my savings quickly dwindled following the purchases for the flat, rent, and bills. I was just managing to keep my head above water, still waiting to start my job in primary care, waiting for HR to sign me off.

In December, I started doing some locum shifts for a multi-chain pharmacy. I was enjoying living alone, with lots of bars and restaurants at my fingertips. Then Christmas approached. I was drinking quite heavily at this point. I remember one night, being asleep while Emma was over, and I had to get up in the middle of the night because I had so much red wine, it had started to seep out of my nostril when I was asleep. So, I got up and was sick. This was probably the shock I needed to slow down on the drinking.

As Christmas approached, I found myself at the John Lewis department store every other day, purchasing for others and myself. Then, on Boxing Day, I found myself going to sales at Trafford Centre, a large shopping mall. I remember thinking, *I am not going to buy a new watch*. The best thing to do at this point was to go home. After about half an hour in the mall, I stumbled across the Brietling Boutique. I thought, *There's no harm in going in and having a look*. As I walked in, I immediately spotted a piece I had seen before. The salesman came over to me asked if I would like to have a closer look. At this point, there was no way I was going to buy it. For one, I could not afford it. Anyway, I thought I would play along with the salesman.

The next thing I knew, I was trying on the watch. I definitely did not have the cash in the bank; however, the salesman told me there was a four-year interest-free pay-monthly option. From my previous years' activity financially, I was sure I would be rejected. Anyway, he decided to apply for the loan. But even if it is rejected, you can call up the bank find out why. He asked me to hold on and called the bank. They informed him they needed to ensure my identity and needed my passport. Now I started getting a little excited. I really liked the watch. They told me to get my passport. It was in my car. I came back with it rather quickly. The next thing I knew, I was walking out with an eighteen-karat solid-gold watch. It was done now. This added to my monthly bills.

I took my newly acquired watch and went down to the local pub. I was slightly embarrassed as I told people its cost. This was an impulse purchase, and shopping sprees are a hallmark of people with bipolar disorder. The next thing I knew, I had the brilliant idea to go to Israel. Within no time at all, I had booked a ticket leaving Manchester on 1 January 2020. When I told Emma I was going, she thought it was a bit spontaneous was upset I had not consulted her. On New Year's Day 2020, I boarded the El Al Airline from Manchester Airport to Tel-Aviv. The usual story: I was triple checked by security before being allowed to board the aeroplane. Then, when I arrived in Israel, there were the questions: Why have you come back? I explained I had come to pray, and Jerusalem was the holiest place in the world. After an hour of questioning, they finally let me through border control.

I got a taxi to the hotel. I was not staying at the King David, having not paid the bill last time, so I stayed just around the corner, as I was familiar with the area. I told the taxi I needed to go to Jerusalem to the King David Hotel. It was an Arab taxi driver, and he took me round the houses. It was taking a very long time before I reached my destination. Everyone knows where the King David is. In the end, he dropped me off in the middle of town and told me it was just up the street. He ripped me off! It took me about forty-five minutes to walk to hotel from where he left me.

I was back in Jerusalem, and my first stop, as always while here, was the Wailing Wall. I went down and prayed and took in the atmosphere. Then the evening was upon us, and I tried to find my way back to hotel. I was a little lost, and there seemed to be roadworks everywhere. So, I decided just to follow the people who dressed in traditional rabbinic clothes. I ended up being taken to tomb of King David. I prayed here, too. I was my first visit to his tomb, which was surreal, and I got a real sense of belonging there. Then I made my way back to the hotel to get some rest.

The next day, I went to meet my friends at the jewellery shop across the road from the King David. I did a little shopping, and my friend opened a bottle of Jonnie Walker Gold Label whisky. The next thing I knew, it was six o'clock—time for the shop to shut, and the bottle was emptied. I went back to the Western Wall to pray. I'd had something on my mind for a long time. I wanted God to show the whole world he was the Master and we were feeble in comparison. From nowhere, while at the wall, I shouted, "El Shaddai, El Shaddai, why don't you give the world a sign of your power!" I was sick of this capitalist world. I had not heard of El Shaddai before shouting out to him. It is the Hebrew name for God Almighty, the God of Israel. As I did this, a policeman walked towards me. Then a chief rabbi appeared with man at his side, so I joined in with their prayers, and the policeman left. Then, as the chief rabbi left, I went to touch him; I was told not to, but I manage it, and then he kissed my hand. He gave me a thumbs up. It was almost as if the prayer had been affirmed by the chief rabbi.

The next two days, I spent between the Jewish quarter, Western Wall, and Mamilla, the shopping street. Then it was time to get back to Manchester. I left with plenty of time to get to the airport. This time, I took the train, as locals had warned me about the scamming Arab taxi drivers. When I got to the airport, everything seemed to be going well, not the usual hassle of "Where have you been? What were you doing here?" It was all going well, with plenty of time to spare. Then I was asked to step aside, and they made me wait while they checked a few things. I sat and waited. I looked at my watch. It was eleven o'clock. Then, five minutes later, I looked at my watch again, and it was 11:45 a.m. I explained to the man I had been here forty-five minutes, and he looked puzzled. Then another man sat next to me. He was panicking that we were going to miss the flight. Then a big queue appeared for our flight. Everyone was anxious that they were going to miss the flight. I looked at my watch, and it was 12:30 p.m. We had skipped another forty minutes or so. Everyone had been cheated an hour or so, it seemed, and there was panic among the passengers that we were going to miss the flight. I was calm. I knew we had all checked in and got our boarding passes.

Then the airport official called me up and said, "You're fine to go. Just get in the queue." I gave him a little smile, just to say, *Ha! God has had one over you here!*

I was soon back in Manchester, feeling energized after having a break. Even though it was more of a pilgrimage, on God's duty. I soon got back into the swing of Locums, travelling all around the North of England and North Wales. I was getting by OK. After Israel, I just felt that Emma was not the girl for me, so we called it a day. Then the time came for me to start my new job in primary care. Everything was going well. Then COVID-19 hit. On 11 March 2020, it was declared a pandemic by the World Health Organization.

Suddenly, I was living alone and working alone during lockdown. I felt the pandemic had been totally mismanaged by the government and we should have shut the airports a lot earlier. From having quite an active social life, I was suddenly isolated. From social drinking, I was now drinking at home—beer, wine, spirits, anything I could get my hands on. Lockdown took its toll on me, and my mental health started to decline.

I started hearing voices again, God, Jesus, and Liz from the hotel in Sheffield. Around Easter, which was 12 April 2020, I started to think about God more and more. And on 5 April 2020, I posted on YouTube as Rabbi Atif Yousaf. I was thinking of starting an online church, one that focused on Judaism, Christianity, and Islam. On Easter weekend, everything got a bit too much for me, and I called in sick on Easter Monday, the day I was supposed to be at work.

I was finding it increasingly difficult to cope living on my own, hearing all these voices. Then I started thinking that people could hear my thoughts again. The pandemic was going from bad to worse. I even started my oral aripiprazole, but it had little effect. The voices and paranoia were worse than ever. My sleep went out of the window. I was sleeping only four to five hours each night.

One day, for some reason that is not clear to me now, I decided to visit the queen and Prince Phillip at Windsor. One morning, I decided to head down to Windsor. This was all happening during a universal travel ban. I made it down to Windsor early in the morning for about 8 a.m. I parked at the church just on the high street in the warden's parking space. For some reason, I had decided that day to dress in a suit. I got to the gate of Windsor Castle and asked the police to speak to the king. They said, there's no king here. So I said, I'll settle for the queen and Prince Philip. After this, I went to walk around the town centre. I remember smashing one of my iPhones on the ground because it was made in China and that's where the pandemic started. So, my rational thinking was non-existent.

Later that day, the police at the castle started asking why I had come to Windsor. I had no good reason. I told them I had come to tell the queen that her government was incompetent and had totally mismanaged the pandemic. They said this was not a matter for the queen, and obviously, I would not be able to see her. They informed me I should go back to Manchester. I told them I did not have any money and had run out of petrol. They told me to go the petrol station and fill out a form enabling me to pay later. Then, they pretty much escorted me out of Windsor.

Then on the way back to Manchester, I got lost. I had done the journey many times, bit still, I seemed to keep going in the wrong direction. All I had to do was head northwest. At some point, I was around Birmingham. My car was running low on petrol, so I went in and asked them if I could fill up, sign a form, and pay later. The lady behind the counter said no, so I filled up anyway and went in to pay with my card. Transaction declined. The attendant did not know what to do. She went to get the manager, at which point, I thought, *Sod this*. I walked and drove away, managing to get myself on the motorway. While travelling up to Manchester, a police motorcycle went past in the fast lane, with emergency lights on but not seeming to be chasing anyone, so I decided to follow him at high speed, but I could not keep up.

Then, one day, in May, I got a missed call from Switzerland, and I was convinced this was from Liz. So the next thing I knew, I was booking a flight on Skyscanner to Switzerland. The flight I managed to book was via Dusseldorf. I booked a hotel in Switzerland. I turned up for my flight, and the airport was dead. There were not many flights going anywhere. I got chatting to a person on the same flight as me. He said everyone was having trouble downloading boarding passes. He informed me that he was travelling for work, which was essential, and he needed a note from his employer to fly. I lied and told him I was flying abroad to do some research as a pharmacist for a vaccine. I did not have a face mask either, but they gave me one as I boarded the airplane.

As we were about to touch down in Germany, I was handed an arrival form. I informed the steward I was getting a connecting flight. She said, "Fill it in, anyway."

We landed in Dusseldorf. I went to the immigration with my half-completed form, they let me through, and I went to departures. Here, I kept up the lie about being a researcher. However, I was told I would not be able to travel onwards, as the Swiss would need a letter for my purpose of travel from my employer. So far, I had just been using my NHS badge, saying I was working for them.

I was stranded in Germany, with no way to get back. My return flight was from Zurich to Amsterdam to Manchester. I managed to book a hotel while waiting for a bus to the city centre. At first, I booked the hotel for only two nights. When I got to the hotel, it was very basic but conveniently centrally located. I asked if I could book for another two nights, using cash. The lady at the desk agreed. I went walking around the city centre, just sightseeing. Most places were closed now, in partial lockdown. I managed to find a Bang Olufsen shop. I had their headphones and went in to enquire about other products. However, I became quite friendly with the assistant, Alex, and we became friends. I would go into the shop, and we would talk about politics, among other things. One day, we went into the local park and enjoyed a bottle of whisky. All this time, I was hearing voices.

I was running out of money, and I would find myself wandering around the city at all times of the day and night. I would continuously get lost. I would turn on my Google maps, but that would have me going round in circles. Nothing seemed to be going right for me in Dusseldorf. Then my brother booked a flight for me back to Manchester. It was due to depart at 11 a.m. I got to the airport with plenty of time. When I got there, the only flight departing was 1 p.m., so I took my time and thought I must be on the 1 p.m. flight. When I went to go through to the gate, they informed me that boarding had finished for my flight and I had missed it. There was no room on the later 1 p.m. flight. Then, when I enquired why my flight was not on the information notice boards, they said it was. I went back to the notice board, and they had put my flight on one side and the other flight on the other side.

Anyway, I was stuck in Dusseldorf. I contacted my friend from university, Jaz. He helped me out, organizing a new flight for me and transferring some money to keep me going. I had asked him to get me a flight to London. He managed to get me a flight a couple of days later. I was struggling to get accommodation and spent one night on the streets and in the airport. Other concerned friends also tried to help me out. I managed to get accommodation for the last night of my unscheduled stay in Dusseldorf. I was the only resident in the hotel and was staying on the twentieth floor. All in all, I was in Dusseldorf for nine days. It was a beautiful city, and I did a lot of window shopping in designer shops.

I managed to get my flight from Dusseldorf to London, which was via Zurich. When I landed at Zurich, to get the transfer to London, they looked at my passport at the check-in point and asked which city I was born in. On my birth certificate and so far, as I knew I had been born in Manchester. They told me to wait a while whilst they checked this out. They came back to me later and said, "We have you down as born in Stockport." He also advised, "Next time you're asked, say Stockport."

I thought this was bizarre. I boarded the flight to London Heathrow. When the flight got to Heathrow, there was an announcement: "Could Mohammad Atif Yousaf please disembark the airplane first. All other passengers please remain seated."

I departed the airplane, and waiting for me were the police. My phone had run out of battery, and I could not get hold of my friend Faisal, who was picking me from the airport. The police questioned me for a while and then just let me go. My friend had gone back home. Then I got a Black Cab to his house, which thankfully, he paid for on the other end. I asked him if I could borrow some money, which he kindly facilitated. Then

I asked for him to drop me off in Windsor. I stayed at the Harte and Garter Hotel on the high street, just opposite the castle. However, by now, I was very ill and walking round the streets, acting oddly. Still, at this time, I had the notion people could hear my thoughts.

I must have shouted out something that offended a young girl, something against the Catholic religion. The girl followed me, and I ran away. Eventually, I got back to the hotel, and they must have heard that I had been acting in a bizarre manner, as they asked me to leave.

I had been in contact with my friend Dan from theological college. He realized I needed some help and offered that I live with him. I accepted, but by this time, things had spun way out of control. Dan fetched me from Windsor, and we went back to his house in Gloucester. I had also been in contact with another friend, Ed. He had also come to Dan's to offer me some support. The support I got from Dan was amazing. A few days went by, and things were getting better. I had somebody looking after me, which felt good. I felt secure and safe with Dan. Then came another important issue: I needed some belongings from my flat in Manchester.

Ed drove me up to Manchester, and we first went to my parents' house, where my car was parked. I asked my mother for the car keys. I took the car, and we went to my flat and took the essentials. I made my way back to Gloucester. Looking back, the biggest mistake I made was getting my car back. Dan did his best to try and contain my driving to a minimum, but I was in a poor frame of mind. I was driving all over. One or two days, I went into Oxford and visited Blenheim Palace. Another day, I ended up in London. I remember I was so sleep-deprived, driving had become very difficult, and I hit the kerb on many occasions. I was getting stopped by police left, right, and centre. Each time, they let me go.

A couple of days, I went to Bristol and tried buying a Porsche. One day, while driving down the motorway, birds were flying across the road, and one of them smashed into my windscreen. Suddenly, I felt as if I needed to be back in Manchester. All along, I had the notion of the girl called Liz from the Sheffield Hotel, so I proceeded to stop at that hotel for a couple of days. I told them I was doing locums. From there, I visited Bridlington and started to visit Chatsworth House and surrounding areas, most frequently the town of Bakewell, Derbyshire.

Before I knew it, the local police were on my back. I ended up following a car, driving very slowly behind it and occasionally shunting it very lightly. In my mind, it was Liz driving it. Then the police came, cornering my car with three or four police cruisers. I was taken into custody for the night. Then the next day, I ended up travelling from Manchester back to Chatsworth, again wearing a suit. I sat on the grass, where others were also enjoying the sun. The difference was I was drinking whisky. Then I apparently, I started shouting loudly, which alarmed other people in the vicinity. Then Chatsworth security came. I threw my keys at them and said, look after these. I can't drive. Then the police came and took me away. Another night in the cells, charged with public order offence. Then, while in the cell, I asked for a Quran. As I did not fully agree with what was written in there, I ripped pages out and flushed them down the toilet. Then I asked for a Bible. Again, because I wasn't too happy with the way the Apostle Paul had steered Christianity away from Judaism, I ripped out the letters from Paul and flushed them down the toilet too. This gave me a charge of criminal damage. I still had not been assessed by the mental health team, but I was let go to appear in court later.

The next day, not having learnt my lesson, I was back in Chatsworth. During the day, I just chilled out in the park area. Then I spent some time in Bakewell. I was standing outside my car, playing music loudly in a car park, when a community support officer came up to me and started asking me questions. I got in my car, but it would start, so I ran away from him. He continued following me. I ran back to the car said a prayer, and it started. I drove away later. Then, for some reason, I thought I would go back to Chatsworth at night. I got out of the car at Chatsworth at night and started hitting a sign with my hockey stick.

I thought I had better head back to Manchester. I was driving away from Chatsworth towards Bakewell when I saw a police car going towards Chatsworth. I thought, *He's going to be after me.* Then I looked in the rearview mirror, and there was the police car, flashing its lights. No siren, though. For some bizarre reason, because I felt harassed by them and because I was ill, I decided to myself I was not going to stop. When we got to the open roads, I put my foot down in my little Nissan Micra. The police could not keep up with me, so I kept slowing down to see if they were still in pursuit. I was rally driving round corners dangerously. The chase went on for nearly twenty minutes. Then I crossed a roundabout, and the police were waiting for me with stingers. I sped up; the second stinger seemed to the trick, and my car came to a standstill. I was taken back to Chesterfield Police Station. I remember one policeman shouting at me. By now, I knew I was in trouble. Anyway, this time, the police had decided to take me Chesterfield Hospital and their mental health section.

I spent four months in hospital at Chesterfield. When I came out, I had to move back in with my parents. A few days later, I was charged with dangerous driving. I was handed a two-year driving ban.

On reflection, God has made himself known to myself. However, this, in turn, has contributed to my mania.

If I am a prophet, I believe God will judge us for our deeds and the way we treat each other and our world. It does not matter what religion you are, mostly because we inherit these traits from our family. What matters is that we live peacefully and respect each other. However, if you do get to know and follow Jesus, that is a bonus, because he is the Son of God and a real superhero.

Printed in the United States
by Baker & Taylor Publisher Services